Rejuvenated
JEWELS

BEVERLY MASSACHUSETTS

QUARRY BOOKS

JUL 2009

Rejuvenated JEWELS

New Designs from
Vintage Treasures

Amy Hanna

First published in the United States of America in 2009 by
Quarry Books, a member of
Quayside Publishing Group
100 Cummings Center
Suite 406-L
Beverly, Massachusetts 01915-6101
Telephone: (978) 282-9590
Fax: (978) 283-2742
www.quarrybooks.com

Library of Congress Cataloging-in-Publication Data

Hanna, Amy.
Rejuvenated jewels : new designs from vintage treasures /
Amy Hanna. -- 1st ed.
p. cm.
Includes index.
ISBN 978-1-60059-313-0 (pb - trade pbk. : alk. paper)
1. Jewelry making. 2. Costume jewelry. I. Title.
TT212.H39 2009
745.594'2--dc22

2008012948

ISBN-13: 978-1-59253-535-4
ISBN-10: 1-59253-535-6

10 9 8 7 6 5 4 3 2 1

Printed in China

Red Lips 4 Courage Communications, Inc.
www.redlips4courage.com

Eileen Cannon Paulin
President

Catherine Risling
Director of Editorial

Editor: Rebecca Ittner
Copy Editors: Christine Allen-Yazzie, Catherine Risling
Art Director: Jocelyn Foye
Production Designers: Liz King, Jocelyn Foye
Illustrator: Pam Garrison
Photographers: Mark Tanner,
Eddie Martinez (pages 3, 10, 14, 17, 20, 21)
Cover Photographer: Zachary Williams

Contents

Introduction

A Creative Journey

I grew up in a small town in Michigan in a close-knit, loving family where imagination was nurtured and creativity abounded. I feel fortunate to have people in my life who have loved, encouraged, and inspired me. Their support helped launch my creative journey.

When I was a little girl, I would sometimes stay overnight with one of my aunts. It was there that I first fell in love with jewelry. She would let me browse through the big cedar jewelry box that sat on her dresser and sometimes she would let me take a piece home. Another aunt gave me an old satin jewelry box filled with vintage rhinestone jewelry. That was a life-changing day. As I sat staring at the sparkly gems, something inside of me lit up.

Throughout my life I have had the urge to create and I have enjoyed working in various mediums. I've always loved jewelry, but have had a difficult time finding pieces that I love. While antiquing I found some special elements that inspired me to create my own designs using vintage jewelry. I am happy to give these vintage beauties a new place to shine.

Like all things, I think jewelry should reflect your personal style. My finished pieces are a mix of textures and colors. I love placing a beautiful gemstone bead next to a vintage medal, or a sparkly rhinestone piece next to an odd-shaped pearl. You'll also notice that my designs are often asymmetrical—a clasp may end up on the front of a necklace, or the length of chains won't be the same on each side.

When I told one of my closest friends that I was writing a how-to jewelry book featuring my designs, she posed an important question: "What do you want to share with your readers?" Her question made me stop and think. Did I want this book to teach people how to wire wrap? No. Did I want this book to teach people

how to oxidize silver? No. Did I want this book to teach people to use their creativity, to not be afraid to take chances, and to believe in themselves? Yes! Though this is not a technique book, I have included all necessary how-to information to complete the projects, including wire-wrapping and oxidizing.

It is my most sincere wish that by reading this book you will be encouraged and inspired to look at your forgotten or unused jewelry, gems, and beads in a new light and give them a fresh start.

Hunting for individual pieces to use in rejuvenated jewelry can be just as much fun as the process of creating each necklace, bracelet, or earring. Over the years I have found that flea markets provide a wealth of vintage baubles. I have had the most luck digging through old cigar boxes and timeworn velvet boxes.

I went to my first flea market more than twenty years ago in Memphis, Tennessee, and fell in love with the experience. The first time I attended a flea market in Paris, I thought I had died and gone to heaven. It has taken me years to collect my wonderful pieces and I am grateful that this book allows me to preserve these beauties and share them with you.

Because the projects in this book are made using mostly vintage items, the pieces you create will not be exact replicas of the ones pictured.

Antique stores and family attics often reveal a bounty of vintage pieces. You can also find many of the same types of vintage beads, pearls, chains, pendants, medals, and more by shopping the easy, no-stress way—online. You'll be happily surprised with what can be found on the Internet.

I realize that not everyone has the time, inclination, or budget to hunt for vintage pieces. The good news is that every project in this book can be made using new items found in craft and bead stores, at bead shows, or through online searches. Where necessary, I give alternatives to the hard-to-find vintage items used in the projects.

In the following chapters, you will learn the jewelry-making techniques necessary to turn your baubles and trinkets into beautiful, unique necklaces, bracelets, and earrings to wear every day. So, go ahead, rejuvenate your jewelry.

Amy Hanna

Chapter 1

Getting Started

This chapter introduces the vast array of beads, found items, findings, materials, and tools needed to create the jewelry featured in this book. You also will learn the simple jewelry-making techniques required to make each of the projects.

I have some favorite things that I reach for time and again when making jewelry. These include pearls and rhinestones of all sizes and shapes; watch fobs; chains; ornate Victorian clasps, lockets, pins, and brooches; gemstones and glass beads; and Paris-styled cameos, charms, and medals.

When looking for vintage pieces to use in your projects, there are a few things to keep in mind. Look for the pretty parts contained in each piece of jewelry. You might not like the finished piece, but there may be exquisite beads, rhinestones, or pearls on it. Also, don't

hesitate to purchase broken pieces of jewelry. Sometimes those little bits contain beautiful clasps, chain pieces, or charms. Once you get them home, you can take them apart and use the pieces you do like.

Before beginning any project, you should prepare your work space. Work on a flat, steady surface with good lighting. To minimize eyestrain, use a task light with a built-in magnifier and keep tools within easy reach. Lay a bead cloth or a piece of velvet on your work surface to prevent small items from rolling around or bouncing off.

It is helpful to practice the wire-wrapping techniques prior to working on any of the projects. To save money, use craft wire when you practice. Once you feel comfortable with the techniques, creating the designs shown in this book will be a breeze.

Beads, Pearls & Rhinestones

Beads

Many colors, sizes, and types of beads are available. My favorite place to purchase them is at bead shows—the prices are great and the selection is unbeatable.

Czech glass and crystal beads

Czech glass and crystal beads are available in many colors, shapes, and sizes. They comprise a basic component of many of these projects.

Gemstone beads

Though many people are drawn to polished, flawless gemstone beads, I prefer those with a chunky shape and a flat finish or unusual tint. My favorites are garnets, rubies, and sapphires. Appetite and black onyx beads are also lovely. (See photo A.)

Mercury glass beads

Vintage mercury glass beads are rare and very delicate; they are my absolute favorite. I love the discoloration they acquire over time. They break very easily, so look for thicker beads to use in your creations and use extreme care when working with them. If they are used on a piece that will be given as a gift or sold, be sure to inform the new owner that the beads are delicate and sometimes irreplaceable.

When you come across mercury beads at a reasonable price, don't hesitate to buy them. I once purchased many mercury glass beads from a dealer who had removed them from a 1920s flapper dress. I have even found them on old Christmas decorations. Once in a while I'll hit the jackpot and find an old necklace made with some precious mercury beads. (See photo B.)

Mother-of-pearl beads

Mother-of-pearl beads come in many shapes
and sizes. I collect old rosaries made with
mother-of-pearl beads. The rosaries can be
taken apart and the beads used individually
or in strands. (See photo C.)

Pearls

Pearls have been used throughout history to
symbolize power and wealth. They are said
to represent purity and fidelity. Personally, I
think pearls possess an almost magical quality.
While most people look for pearls with lots of
luster, a smooth surface, and a perfectly round
shape, I am drawn to pearls that have little
bumps, blemishes, cracks, or spots. In fact,
the more bumps and discoloration the pearls
reveal, the more I love them. Pearls come in a
wide range of colors, from off-white, yellow,
and pink to blue, green, gray, and black. I use
a variety of pearl types, including baroque,
keishi, rice, and stick.

Baroque pearls

Baroque pearls are irregularly shaped and can be
freshwater, saltwater, cultured, natural, or faux.
My favorite baroque pearls are vintage Miriam
Haskell faux pearls. Her original pieces, made
from the mid-1920s through the 1940s, were
sought after by such celebrities as Joan Crawford
and Lucille Ball. Because Haskell always worked
with the best materials, such as Murano glass
faceted crystals from Austria and lustrous faux
pearls from Japan, her original pieces remain
very collectible. (See photo D.)

Keishi pearls

Keishi pearls are formed when the mollusk ejects
the pearl bead nucleus but continues to make a
pearl. I use these little pearls on earrings and with
connectors on necklaces and bracelets. (See photo E.)

Rice and seed pearls

Rice pearls are small, oval pearls that have been drilled through lengthwise. (See photo F.) Seed pearls are small, round pearls that measure no larger than 2 mm.

Stick pearls

Stick pearls are long and thin and have many irregularities. The striking shapes add an elegant, unique look to jewelry. (See photo G.)

Rhinestones

Rhinestones are available in many forms and sizes (see photos H & I). Rhinestone beads, brooches, chains, clasps, and dangles can be found on vintage necklaces, bracelets, and earrings.

If you use new rhinestone pieces in these projects, you will need to oxidize them to achieve an aged look (see Using Oxidizing Solution, page 20).

Consider purchasing loose rhinestones whenever you run across them at flea markets or antique stores. I have been fortunate to find baggies full of different sizes and colors. When working with vintage rhinestone pieces, you will often discover spaces with missing rhinestones. By having a stash of loose rhinestones on hand, you can doctor pieces as necessary.

Findings

Here you will find a list of the types of findings used in the projects in the following chapters. Please note that silver-colored findings are available in both sterling silver and base metal. I use sterling silver findings because they oxidize well and can stand the test of time.

New chains are available as finished pieces and are also sold by the foot. Because I often mix different types of chain when creating a piece of jewelry, I make sure to have a variety on hand. (See photo J.)

Bracelets and chains

Vintage charm bracelets are great to have on hand. I refashion them by adding beads, rhinestones, or pictures to the existing bracelet.

New bracelet bases are available in a wide range of styles and can be found in bead and craft stores and through Internet searches.

Vintage chains abound at flea markets and antique stores. Be sure to have various types, lengths, and thicknesses on hand, including cable chain, crystal chain, rhinestone chain, rosary chain, and watch chain.

Clasps and closures

Though my favorite way to finish a necklace is with a vintage rhinestone clasp, just about anything can be made into a clasp or closure. You can always use a clasp as intended, but I like to think outside of the box. Old hooks can be used to attach vintage rhinestone brooches to necklaces or bracelets. Lobster claws work with most any style of ring. (See photo K.)

I use a variety of closures on my designs including hook-and-eye closures, lobster claw clasps, spring rings, and toggle clasps.

Connectors

Connectors are available in a wide variety of materials, shapes, and sizes. New connectors are easily found in bead and craft stores and through Internet searches. I prefer using vintage connectors and have great luck finding them on pieces of vintage religious jewelry. In addition to connectors, I use pins and rings to attach pieces together. (See photo L.)

Crimp beads

Crimp beads are small, seamless metal beads or tubes used to securely hold wires and chains together or to hold beads in place on wire. (See photo M3.)

Ear wires

Ear wires are used to create earrings for pierced ears and to enable a bead or drop to be attached. (See photo M2.)

Head pins

Used to make bead drops, a head pin is a short piece of straight wire with a small ornament on one end that prevents a bead or gemstone from falling off. To add a bit of drama to your jewelry, use head pins that have decorative ends such as rhinestones, balls, or squares. (See photo M1.)

Jump rings

A jump ring is a small oval or round wire ring that can be opened and closed to link jewelry parts together. (See photo M2.)

Metal wire

Wire is sized in gauges. The lower the number, the thicker the wire. Metal types available include brass, copper, fine silver, gold, gold-filled, and sterling silver. You will need round sterling silver wire in 20- to 26-gauge for these projects. (See photo M5.)

Nylon-coated, stainless steel bead-stringing wire

This strong, flexible wire is used to make necklaces and bracelets. This type of wire is available in various colors and diameters.

Found Objects

In addition to beads and findings, I use a multitude of found objects in my designs including pins, reliquaries, charms, and tintypes.

Cameos

Cameos hold a special place in my heart; I have loved them since I was a little girl. Vintage cameos can be found at estate sales, antique stores, flea markets, and jewelry stores that specialize in antique jewelry. New cameos can be found in bead stores and through Internet searches. (See photo N.)

Charms

I use charms in most of my pieces. Vintage charms are easy to find and collect, and new ones can be found in bead, craft, and jewelry stores.

Decorative paper and mica

I use small pieces of vintage decorative paper in lockets and pendants. Mica can be used instead of glass in lockets and on watch faces. (See photo O.)

Pendants

Pendants can be made from just about anything. One necklace I made had a silly rubber lemon man as the pendant. I have also made a pendant by attaching rubies and a silver bird charm to a shell. Watch fobs, religious relics, medals, cameos, lockets, watches, and stones make wonderful pendants. (See photo P.)

Tintypes

A tintype is a positive photograph made by a collodion process on a thin iron plate, resulting in a darkened surface. I have had great luck finding these small photographs in vintage photo albums found at antique stores and flea markets, and through Internet searches. (See photo Q.)

Materials & Tools

To complete the projects in this book, you will need to have the following materials and tools.

Adhesives

Three types of adhesives are used on the projects in this book: craft glue, dimensional glue, and jewelry cement. Craft glue is used to adhere ephemera and ribbon to lockets and pendants. Dimensional glue dries to a clear-glass finish and is used to glue beads in place. Jewelry cement is used to attach beads, pearls, and rhinestones and dries clear. I use regular and quick-drying jewelry cement.

Anvil

An anvil is a heavy iron block on which metal is marked or shaped.

Awl

An awl is used to pierce small holes in metal and leather.

Center punch

A center punch is typically used as an aid to drilling. A drill, when brought into contact with a flat surface, will have a tendency to wander on the surface until it gains sufficient contact to start cutting a hole. A center punch forms a small dimple in the surface. The tip of the drill will sit in the dimple, thus preventing the drill from wandering.

Clamp

A clamp is used to hold small jewelry pieces in place while they are drilled or as adhesive dries.

Crimping pliers

Crimping pliers are used to close crimp beads. The pliers provide a much smaller crimp than flat-nose pliers.

Flat-nose pliers

Flat-nose pliers have a flat interior jaw and a box nose. They are used to bend and pull wire. You will need to have two pairs on hand when wire wrapping.

Jewelry file

This fine-grit metal file is used to smooth edges or burs in wire or metal.

Oxidizing solution

Oxidizing solution is used to give a dark, aged patina to sterling silver. Read instructions prior to using and wear rubber gloves and safety glasses when working with the solution.

Rotary drill

A rotary drill is used to bore holes in a variety of surfaces. It can be handheld or used with an optional accessory drill press.

Round-nose pliers

Round-nose pliers have cylindrical jaws that taper to a point at the nose. They are used to create loops in head pins and wire.

Rubber gloves and safety glasses

Rubber gloves and safety glasses must be worn when using oxidizing solution. Safety glasses should also be worn when using a drill and when clipping wire.

Scissors

Scissors are used to cut bead wire and trim decorative paper, mica, and tintypes. I like to have a variety of sizes on hand.

Wire cutters

Wire cutters are used to cut heavier wire and head pins. They can also be used to remove pin backs and button shanks.

In addition to the materials and tools listed, you may want to consider having the following on hand:

- Bead reamer: Used to enlarge holes in beads to allow room for wire.

- Buffing tool: Used to remove fingerprints and give shine to jewelry.

- Resealable bags: Used to store individual elements as well as projects in progress.

- Tweezers: Used to pick up small beads, jump rings, etc.

Techniques

Following are the techniques used to create the jewelry in this book. If you are new to jewelry-making, consider practicing the wire-wrapping techniques prior to beginning any of the projects. To save money, use craft wire while practicing wire wrapping techniques.

Using Oxidizing Solution

Before using any sterling silver chain, wire, or pendant, I oxidize it to take away the shine and to give each piece a dark, aged patina. The only exception is if the piece already has an aged look. I oxidize a few items at a time.

When oxidizing silver, be sure to allow yourself enough time to finish the process. It is important to keep an eye on the pieces in the solution; be sure you do not over-oxidize them. If left in the solution too long the pieces will rust, so you do not want to get distracted.

It is important to note that oxidizing solution is highly toxic. Do not use the solution around children or pets. Oxidizing must be done in a well-ventilated space—it is best to work outside. Always wear rubber gloves and safety goggles when working with oxidizing solution. I recommend wearing an apron. Use medium-sized plastic bowls with a lid (I use the disposable kind from the grocery store). For safety purposes, label the contents of one of the bowls with a permanent marker.

Instructions

1. Wearing rubber gloves and safety glasses, pour approximately 2 cups (0.47 liter) of warm water into the labeled bowl. Add 2 tablespoons (29.57 ml) of oxidizing solution. In the other disposable bowl, add 3 cups (0.71 liter) of warm water. You will use this water to rinse the oxidized pieces.

2. You will need to test a piece of jewelry in the oxidizing solution to make sure the solution is the right strength. Dip one piece in the solution and watch its progress. If it does not start to darken after a couple of minutes, you may need to add more solution to the water. The longer you leave the silver piece in the oxidizing solution, the darker it will become.

3. Once the desired color is achieved, remove the piece from the oxidizing solution and rinse it in the bowl of warm water. Dry the oxidized piece with a clean paper towel. *Note:* If your

piece gets too dark, don't fret. In a small bowl, mix powdered laundry detergent with a small amount of water to make a paste. Rub the paste on the oxidized piece with a soft cloth. This will usually remove the dark patina.

Oxidizing the Natural Way

If you prefer a nontoxic way to age your pieces, you can use freshly boiled eggs to do the job. First, hard boil a few eggs. While they are still warm, discard the shells and break up the eggs in a bowl. Immediately put the eggs in a plastic bag, along with the piece you want to age. Gently move the piece around, making sure to coat it with the eggs. Leave the piece in the bag with the eggs until it achieves the patina you desire. Remove the piece from the bag and rinse it well in cool water. Gently dry the piece with a clean paper towel. Be aware that this method does not give the even results achieved with other oxidation methods.

Preparing Found Objects

Snip off the pin back or button shank using wire cutters. Smooth the cut edges with a jewelry file.

Using a Rotary Drill

I have a handheld rotary drill with an accessory drill press; I use them to create holes in pieces when necessary.

When choosing a drill-bit size, consider the size of the piece to be drilled and the gauge of wire you will be using; I typically use either a ¾₄-inch (0.5 cm) or ¹⁄₁₆-inch (0.16 cm) bit. When drilling through metal, use a center punch to mark your spot prior to drilling. This will prevent the drill bit from wandering off your mark.

If the piece you are drilling is too small to be clamped down, use a small pair of flat-nose pliers to hold the piece in place while drilling. Be sure to wear safety glasses when operating a drill.

Working with Wire, Head Pins, and Crimp Beads

The techniques shown here will teach you how to create the connecting loops needed to make the projects on the following pages.

Be sure to choose the appropriate gauge wire for the project you are working on. The heavier the jewelry piece, the smaller gauge wire you will want to use. For instance, when working with small beads you will want either 24- or 26-gauge wire. When making an "S" hook closure, or when working with a heavy bead or pendant, you should consider working with 22-gauge wire.

When choosing beads for your necklace or bracelet, make sure the beads at the beginning and end of the piece have larger holes because you will be running two lengths of wire through those beads.

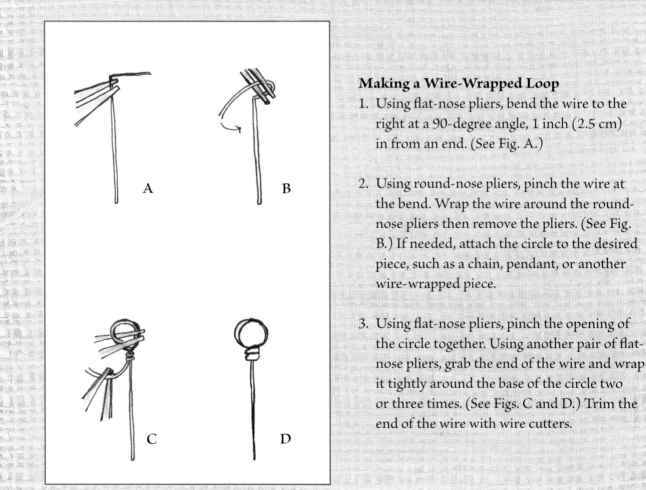

Making a Wire-Wrapped Loop

1. Using flat-nose pliers, bend the wire to the right at a 90-degree angle, 1 inch (2.5 cm) in from an end. (See Fig. A.)

2. Using round-nose pliers, pinch the wire at the bend. Wrap the wire around the round-nose pliers then remove the pliers. (See Fig. B.) If needed, attach the circle to the desired piece, such as a chain, pendant, or another wire-wrapped piece.

3. Using flat-nose pliers, pinch the opening of the circle together. Using another pair of flat-nose pliers, grab the end of the wire and wrap it tightly around the base of the circle two or three times. (See Figs. C and D.) Trim the end of the wire with wire cutters.

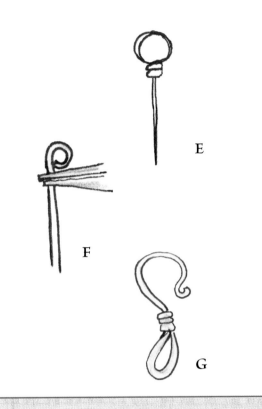

Making a Hook Closure

1. Cut one 2- to 3-inch (5.1 cm to 7.6 cm) piece of wire. Make a wire-wrapped loop at one end. (See Fig. E.)

2. Using round-nose pliers, pinch the opposite end of the wire then roll the wire to form a small circle. (See Fig. F.)

3. Remove the round-nose pliers then pinch them against the wire at the bottom of the circle with the circle facing up. Bend the wire around the fattest part of the round-nose pliers, making a horseshoe shape. (See Fig. G.)

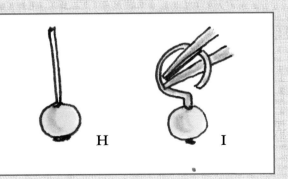

Making a Bead Dangle

1. Thread desired beads onto a head pin. (See Fig. H.)

2. Using round-nose pliers, pinch the top of the wire. (See Fig. I.) Roll the wire around the pliers, forming a complete circle. Remove the pliers.

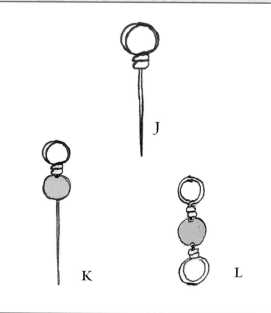

Wire Wrapping a Bead

1. Choose the gauge of wire that will fit through the bead you will wire wrap. Slip the bead onto a piece of wire. Using wire cutters, cut the wire, leaving a 1-inch (2.5 cm) tail of wire on either side of the bead. Remove the bead from the wire. Make a wire-wrapped loop on one end of the wire. (See Fig. J.)

2. Slide the bead onto the wire, making sure it is flush against the wire-wrapped end. (See Fig. K.) Make a wire-wrapped loop at the opposite side of the bead. (See Fig. L.)

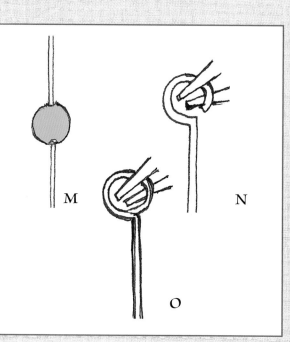

Making a Single-Loop Connector

1. Choose the gauge of wire that will fit through the bead. Slip the bead onto a length of wire. Using wire cutters, cut the wire, leaving a ⅜-inch (0.9 cm) tail of wire on either side of the bead. (See Fig. M.) Remove the bead from the wire.

2. Roll the wire around the pliers, forming a complete circle. Remove the pliers. Using round-nose pliers, pinch the top of the wire. (See Fig. N.)

3. Using flat-nose pliers, pinch the circle closed. (See Fig. O.)

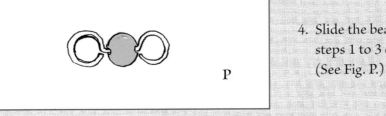

P

4. Slide the bead onto the wire and repeat steps 1 to 3 on the opposite side to finish. (See Fig. P.)

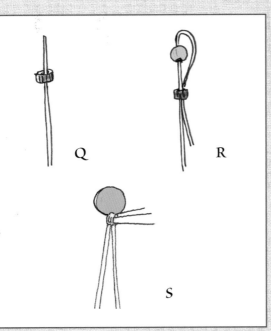

Q

R

S

Working with Crimp Beads
1. String the crimp bead at the end of flexible beading wire. (See Fig. Q.)

2. String the clasp or connector and then pass the end of the wire back through the crimp bead. (See Fig. R.)

3. With the wires side-by-side in the crimp bead, use crimping pliers to flatten the bead. (See Fig. S.) Test the wires to make sure they do not slip through the crimp bead.

Working with Jump Rings
In a side-to-side motion, twist the jump ring open using two sets of flat-nose pliers. (See Fig. T.)

T

Cameos Revisited

My mother has always adored cameos. She once told me that the only thing stopping Mona Lisa from being pure perfection was the fact that she was not wearing a cameo. Over the years I have come to share her appreciation of the delicate features and unique personalities portrayed in cameos.

Authentic cameos have hand-carved images ranging from women, men, and families to flowers, animals, and more. Over the centuries, cameos have been made from assorted materials including agate, coral, lava, shell, mother-of-pearl, and various gemstones.

Important women of history, including Queen Elizabeth and Catherine the Great, adored cameos. However, cameos experienced their greatest resurgence in popularity in the Victorian era. Queen Victoria's fondness

for them fueled the demand for cameos on pendants, pins, rings, and earrings. Authentic cameos are still made today and can be found in jewelry stores and though Internet searches.

Reproduction and mass-produced cameos are widely available in everything from glass and acrylic to plastic. Though these are less expensive than vintage cameos, they lack the hand-carved elegance and beautiful patina found on antique pieces.

The projects in this chapter feature some of my favorite vintage cameos. In one, a unique music box cameo is mixed with rhinestones, pearls, and rubies to create a necklace that's a fresh take on vintage. Another necklace blends dainty crystals and cameos, while rhinestones and cameos work together on a beautiful pair of earrings.

Queen of Cameos Necklace

I love old Queen Victoria commemorative medals. Though most were coin-shaped, the one shown here was made in the shape of a Victorian cross. When I found this medal, it was missing the photograph of Queen Victoria so I used a Victorian cameo in its place. The rhinestone pieces are from an old bracelet; they add just the right amount of sparkle.

Instructions

1. Glue the shell cameo onto the medal with jewelry cement. Use a clamp to hold the cameo in place until the cement is completely dry.

2. Thread two 3 mm ruby gemstone beads onto a head pin and wire wrap the head pin onto the top right side of the medal. Repeat on the top left side of the medal. *Note:* Make sure the beads show in front of the medal.

Beads

- baroque pearls: 15 mm (2)
- crystal beads: 10 mm (2)
- garnet gemstone beads: 18 mm (2)
- rhinestone dangles: 3 mm (8)
- ruby gemstone beads: 3 mm (4)
- ruby zircon beads: 10 mm (2)
- stick pearls: 20 mm (2)

Findings & Found Objects

- medal: 37 mm
- rhinestone bracelet pieces: 3¼ inches (8.2 cm) long (2)
- rhinestone clasp: 2-to-2 strand, 15 mm
- shell cameo: 15 mm
- sterling silver head pins (2)
- sterling silver wire: 24-gauge

Materials & Tools

- clamp
- jewelry cement
- pliers: flat-nose, round-nose
- wire cutters

Alternative Materials

Any type of medal can be used in this project—just be sure the medal is larger than your cameo. Academic, athletic, and military medals are easy to find. Did a relative serve in the armed forces? Has your child received a medal at school? A look through your family memorabilia might just yield the perfect medal.

3. Wire wrap one end of a vintage rhinestone bracelet piece to the top right side of the medal.

4. Wire wrap one crystal bead to the other end of the vintage rhinestone bracelet piece, then make a wire-wrapped loop at the opposite end of the crystal bead.

5. Wire wrap one baroque pearl to the crystal bead, then make a wire-wrapped loop at the opposite end of the baroque pearl.

6. Wire wrap one zircon bead to the baroque pearl, then make a wire-wrapped loop at the opposite end of the zircon bead.

7. Wire wrap one stick pearl to the zircon bead, then make a wire-wrapped loop at the opposite end of the stick pearl.

8. Wire wrap one garnet gemstone bead to the stick pearl, then make a wire-wrapped loop at the opposite end of the garnet gemstone bead.

9. Cut a 3-inch (7.6 cm) piece of wire. Wire wrap one end of the wire to the garnet gemstone bead, then make a wire-wrapped loop at the other end of the wire.

10. Cut a 3-inch (7.6 cm) piece of wire. Wire wrap one end of the wire to the top right loop of the rhinestone clasp. In this order, thread the following onto the wire: two rhinestone dangles, the wire loop at the end of the garnet gemstone bead, two more rhinestone dangles. Wire wrap the end of the wire to the bottom right loop of the rhinestone clasp.

11. Repeat steps 3 to 10 on the left side of the necklace to finish the piece.

Lava Cameo & Tintype Bracelet

When I found this bracelet, it was missing a few cameos. Instead of being disheartened or discouraged, I bought it and transformed the bracelet into something more my style by adding a few tintypes. If you ever run across a damaged piece that you just love, take it home and use your imagination to make it over in your style. Lava cameo bracelets can be pricey and hard to find. This project can also be made using a new oval link bracelet base, new cameos, and modern images.

Instructions

1. Cut the tintypes to fit inside the circles on the bracelet.

2. Using fast-drying jewelry cement, glue the tintypes to the circles.

3. Using the jump ring, attach the charm to the bracelet.

Findings & Found Objects
- cameo bracelet
- charm
- jump ring (6 mm)
- tintypes (3)

Materials & Tools
- fast-drying jewelry cement
- flat-nose pliers
- scissors

Music Box Cameo Necklace

This Victorian cameo, one of my most treasured belongings, was found years ago on an antiquing excursion. Upon further inspection I discovered that the cameo is actually a tiny music box. I wanted to turn the precious find into a timeless family heirloom, so I created this necklace. I often wonder who the original owner of the cameo was and how she could have ever let it go.

Instructions

1. Using the 9 mm jump ring, attach one side of the brass connector to the cameo.

2. Using 24-gauge wire, wire wrap one crystal bead to the opposite end of the brass connector. Wire wrap the crystal bead to the bottom of the rhinestone connector.

Beads
- faux pearls: 6 mm (4)
- keishi pearl: 3 mm
- rhinestone disco ball beads (2)
- rhinestone rondelles: 5 mm (2)
- ruby gemstone beads: 3 mm (3)

Findings & Found Objects
- bead caps: 5 mm (4)
- brass connector: 1 strand
- cable chain: 2 mm (1-inch [2.5 cm] piece)
- cameo
- charm
- crystal-bead connectors: 1-to-1 strand, 5 mm (5)
- jump rings: 4 mm (2); 9 mm (1)
- mother-of-pearl round-bead rosary chain (8 links)
- mother-of-pearl square-bead rosary chain (6 links)
- rhinestone chain pieces (6 links)
- rhinestone clasp: 2-to-2 strand, 15 x 50 mm
- rhinestone connector: 2-to-1 strand, 10 x 20 mm
- sterling silver wire: 24-gauge, 26-gauge

Materials & Tools
- pliers: flat-nose, round-nose
- wire cutters

3. Using a 4 mm jump ring, attach three links of rhinestone chain to the top right hook of the rhinestone connector.

4. Attach two crystal bead connectors together, then attach one end to the rhinestone chain.

5. Cut one 4-inch (10.2 cm) piece of 24-gauge wire and wire wrap one end to the second crystal bead connector. In this order, thread the following onto the wire: bead cap, faux pearl, rhinestone rondelle, faux pearl, bead cap. Make a wire-wrapped loop at the end of the wire.

6. Using 24-gauge wire, wire wrap one disco ball bead to the wire-wrapped loop. Wire wrap the opposite side of the disco ball bead to a 3-link piece of the square-bead rosary chain.

7. Open the loop at the end of the square-bead rosary chain and attach it to a 4-link piece of the round-bead rosary chain.

8. Repeat steps 4 to 7 to complete the left side of the necklace.

9. Cut one 4-inch (10.2 cm) piece of 26-gauge wire and wire wrap one end of the wire to the top right ring on the clasp. In this order, thread the following onto the wire: one 3 mm ruby gemstone bead, end of the right side of the necklace, one 3 mm ruby gemstone bead. Wire wrap the end of the wire to the bottom right ring on the clasp.

10. Cut one 4-inch (10.2 cm) piece of 26-gauge wire and wire wrap one end of the wire to the top left ring on the clasp. Thread one keishi pearl and one 3 mm ruby gemstone bead onto the wire. Wire wrap the end of the wire to the end of the left side of the necklace.

11. Using 24-gauge wire, wire wrap one end of the cable chain to the left side of the clasp.

12. Using a 4 mm jump ring, attach the charm to the opposite end of the cable chain.

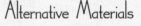

Alternative Materials

Though you may never run across a vintage cameo music box, you can still create a stunning version of this necklace. Choose something beautiful and meaningful to feature on this project, such as a cameo once worn by your grandmother. If you prefer not to use rosary beads, wire wrap mother-of-pearl beads together to achieve the same look.

Cameo & Rhinestone Earrings

Cameos look great when paired with vintage rhinestones and findings. Notice how the silver connectors are different—mixing different shapes of findings is a terrific way to use up all those small, one-of-a-kind pieces. This simple project can be made in less than an hour.

Instructions

1. Using the rotary drill, drill three evenly spaced holes at the bottom of each cameo and two holes at the top. Wire wrap one rhinestone dangle through each hole at the bottom of each cameo.

2. Wire wrap one rhinestone connector through each hole at the top of each cameo.

3. Using jump rings, attach the rhinestone connectors to the silver connectors and the silver connectors to the earring hooks.

Beads
- rhinestone dangles: 4 mm (6)

Findings & Found Objects
- jump rings: 4 mm (4)
- rhinestone connectors: 3 x 20 mm (4)
- shell cameos: 12 x 18 mm (2)
- silver connectors: 2-to-1 strand, 8 mm (2)
- sterling silver earring hooks (2)
- sterling silver wire: 26-gauge

Materials & Tools
- drill bit: 1/32 inch (0.32 cm)
- pliers: flat-nose, round-nose
- rotary drill
- wire cutters

Expert Advice

No Drilling Required

If you don't want to drill through cameos, there is another way to create this project. Glue the cameos to filigree connectors with jewelry cement. The open wirework around the edges of the connectors can easily accommodate wire-wrapped loops and jump rings.

Cameo Locket Necklace

The cameo locket pendant on this necklace is far from perfect—pearls are missing, the gold trim is chipped, and the metal is really oxidized. Notice how the chunky elements of the necklace complement the size of the pendant. When designing your own jewelry, consider how each piece will look next to the other.

Beads

- blue appetite gemstone bead: 18 mm
- blue gemstone bead: 3 mm
- blue glass oval bead: 12 mm
- crystal bead: 10 mm
- green gemstone flat round bead: 8 mm
- green glass oval bead: 18 mm
- green glass square bead: 14 mm
- mother-of-pearl oval bead: 8 mm
- purple gemstone flat round bead: 15 mm
- purple glass bicone bead: 5 x 15 mm
- purple glass long bicone bead: 10 x 45 mm
- rhinestone disco ball beads: 8 mm (1); 14 mm (1)
- rhinestone rondelles: 7 mm (2)
- white keishi pearls: 3 mm (2)

Findings & Found Objects

- blue glass button with shank: 9 mm

- braided cable chain: 5.5 mm (2 inches [5.1 cm])
- brass bead caps: 4 mm (2); 5 mm (2)
- brass charm
- brass connector: 1-to-1 strand, 7 x 10 mm
- cable chain: 4 mm (2 inches [5.1 cm]); 6 mm (1 inch [2.5 cm]); 8 mm (1 inch [2.5 cm])
- cameo locket: 25 x 30 mm
- crystal bead connectors: 1-to-1 strand, 5 mm (4)
- hook closure: 12 mm
- silver crown charm
- silver oval connectors: 1-to-1 strand, 20 mm (2)
- spring clasp: 20 mm
- sterling silver wire: 22-gauge, 24-gauge

Materials & Tools

- pliers: flat-nose, round-nose
- wire cutters

Instructions

1. Using 22-gauge wire, wire wrap the cameo locket to the spring clasp. *Note:* The rest of the necklace will be made using 24-gauge wire.

2. Wire wrap the green gemstone bead to the ring on the spring clasp, then make a wire-wrapped loop at the opposite side of the bead.

3. Cut one 4-inch (10.2 cm) piece of wire and make a loop on one end of the wire. In this order, string the following onto the wire: 4 mm bead cap, purple glass bicone bead, 4 mm bead cap. Make a loop on the opposite end of the wire (see Making a Single-Loop Connector, page 24). Connect one end of the piece to the wire-wrapped loop on the green gemstone bead.

4. Using flat-nose pliers to open and close the loops, link the four crystal bead connectors together. Connect one end to the purple bicone bead piece.

5. Cut one 4-inch (10.2 cm) piece of wire and wire wrap one end to the opposite end of the crystal bead connectors. In this order, string the following onto the wire: keishi pearl, rondelle, 8 mm disco ball bead, rondelle, keishi pearl. Make a wire-wrapped loop at the other side of the bead.

6. Wire wrap the purple gemstone bead to the pearls and rhinestones piece, then wire wrap the opposite side of the purple gemstone bead to the bottom of one silver connector.

7. Wire wrap the blue appetite gemstone bead to the top of the silver connector, then wire wrap the opposite side of the blue appetite gemstone bead to the 10 mm cable chain.

8. Wire wrap the small green gemstone bead to the end of the 10 mm cable chain, then wire wrap the other side of the green gemstone bead to the brass connector and the 6 mm cable chain.

9. Wire wrap the small blue gemstone bead and the crown charm to the end of the 6 mm chain. Wire wrap the charm to the end of the chain.

To make the right side of the necklace:

1. Cut one 5-inch (12.7 cm) piece of wire and wire wrap one end to the left side of the spring clasp. In this order, thread the following onto the wire: bead cap, purple long bicone bead, bead cap. Make a wire-wrapped loop at the opposite side of the purple long bicone bead.

2. Wire wrap the crystal bead to the purple long bicone bead, then make a wire-wrapped loop at the opposite side of the crystal bead. Wire wrap the mother-of-pearl bead to the crystal bead then wire wrap the mother-of-pearl bead to the 8 mm cable chain.

3. Wire wrap one side of the 14 mm disco ball bead to the 8 mm cable chain, then wire wrap the opposite side of the 14 mm disco ball bead to the bottom of a silver connector.

4. Wire wrap one side of the green gemstone bead to the top of the silver connector, then wire wrap the opposite side of the green gemstone bead to the braided cable chain.

5. Wire wrap the end of the braided cable chain to the button shank and the end of the swivel hook.

Alternative Materials

Many of the findings I use, such as connectors, chains, and charms, are from vintage religious jewelry, including the silver connectors found on this necklace. I have always been fascinated by the ornate detail on them. If you have difficulty finding vintage religious jewelry, an Internet search for new religious jewelry findings will provide what you need. Of course, you can always use findings in whatever themes or shapes you desire.

Chapter
3

Souvenirs
& Keepsakes

I find souvenirs from the late 1800s and early 1900s so inspiring. The Victorians created keepsakes with unrivaled craftsmanship and attention to detail. Traveling had become more affordable and accessible to the masses, and travelers longed to bring home souvenirs from their adventures.

In addition to antique souvenirs, I like to use anything French in my pieces. I have collected baubles and trinkets on each trip to Paris and look for French-themed items when hunting closer to home.

Just about anything that reminds a person of a moment in time that was spent at a favorite place or time spent with a special person is a

souvenir. Popular souvenirs for jewelry-making include lockets, pendants, charms, and bracelets.

What favorite memories would you like to capture in a jewelry piece? Shells from a special day at the beach, beads from a necklace that once belonged to a loved one, travel ephemera, and souvenir charms are great jewelry accents. Use what you love; the possibilities are endless.

This chapter features pieces made with vintage souvenirs. The simplest project is a souvenir bracelet accented with beads, pearls, and charms. The most unique project features a vintage shell heart on which I sewed rhinestone connectors.

Simply Sweet Souvenir Bracelet

Beads
- rhinestones: round flat-backed, 3 mm (6)

Findings & Found Objects
- charm
- jump rings: 7 mm (5)
- mother-of-pearl round-bead rosary chain: 4 mm (5 links)
- rhinestone clasp: 2–to-2 strand, 7 x 15 mm
- "S" hook connectors (2)
- souvenir bracelet

Materials & Tools
- fast-drying jewelry cement
- pliers: flat-nose, round-nose

When I buy vintage souvenir bracelets, I often intend to take them apart and use the pieces in a variety of projects. But this bracelet was special—I immediately loved its delicate design and vintage appeal. So I kept the original bracelet intact and simply added some rhinestones and pretty beads and replaced the broken clasp. This simple project is great for someone new to jewelry-making.

Instructions

1. Glue the rhinestones to the center piece of the bracelet.

2. Using jump rings, attach one link of the mother-of-pearl chain to the top and bottom rings on both ends of the links. *Note:* Add more links if you need to make the bracelet longer.

3. Using an "S" hook connector, attach the clasp to the end of the bracelet.

4. Using the second "S" hook connector, attach one link of the mother-of-pearl rosary bead chain to the bottom hook of the clasp. Using a jump ring, attach the charm to the link.

Vintage French Locket Necklace

Most of the time I don't have any idea how I will use a locket or brooch, but I purchase them anyway. Later, when I'm in the studio creating, those bits and pieces somehow come together to lend the perfect touch to a necklace, bracelet, or earrings. I never would have worn this souvenir pin as intended, but I love how it looks on this piece.

Beads

- rhinestone dangles: 4 mm (2)
- sapphire gemstone beads: 5 mm (14); 12 mm (1)

Findings & Found Objects

- bone circle: 14 mm
- brass locket: 30 mm
- cable chain: 3 mm (eight 3-link pieces); 6 mm (two 2½-inch [6.4 cm] pieces); 8 mm (two 3-inch [7.6 cm] pieces)
- charm
- jump ring: 4 mm
- mother-of-pearl oblong-bead rosary chains: 15 mm with ½-inch (1.3 cm) piece of chain attached (2)
- rhinestone connector: 3-to-1 strand, 10 x 20 mm

- silver connectors: 2-to-1 strand, 14 mm (2)
- silver pendant: 10 mm
- souvenir pin with connector ring on the bottom: 12 x 35 mm
- sterling silver head pins (2)
- sterling silver wire: 22-gauge, 24-gauge

Materials & Tools

- clamp
- drill bit: ¼-inch (0.6 cm)
- jewelry cement
- jewelry file
- pliers: flat-nose, round-nose
- rotary drill
- wire cutters

Instructions

1. Using wire cutters, snip the back off the souvenir pin. Smooth any rough edges with a jewelry file.

2. Using a rotary drill, drill one hole in each side of the souvenir pin. *Note:* If your souvenir pin doesn't have a connector ring, drill an additional hole in the center of the bottom of the pin.

3. Using 22-gauge wire, wire wrap the locket to the connector ring on the souvenir pin. Attach the silver pendant to the connector ring with a jump ring.

4. Thread one 5 mm sapphire gemstone bead onto a head pin then wire wrap the head pin through the hole on the right side of the pin. Repeat on the left side of the pin.

5. Using 24-gauge wire, wire wrap one rhinestone dangle through the hole on the right side of the pin. Repeat on the left side of the pin.

6. Using 24-gauge wire, wire wrap the bead of one mother-of-pearl rosary bead chain through the hole on the right side of the pin.

7. Using 24-gauge wire, wire wrap one 12 mm sapphire gemstone bead to the end of the rosary bead chain, then make a wire-wrapped loop at the other end of the sapphire gemstone bead. Repeat two times, attaching the last sapphire gemstone bead to a 3-inch (7.6 cm) piece of 3 mm cable chain. Wire wrap the cable chain to the bottom of a silver connecter.

8. Using 24-gauge wire, wire wrap one ½-inch (1.3 cm) piece of 3 mm cable chain to the top right side of the silver connector.

9. Wire wrap 3-inch (7.6 cm) piece of wire to the end of the 3 mm cable chain. Thread one 5 mm sapphire gemstone bead onto the wire. Wire wrap the end of the wire to a 3-inch (7.6 cm) piece of 8 mm cable chain.

10. Using 22-gauge wire, wire wrap the end of the 8 mm cable chain to the bone circle.

11. Using 24-gauge wire, wire wrap one ½-inch (1.3 cm) piece of 3 mm chain to the top left side of the silver connector.

12. Cut one 3-inch (7.6 cm) piece of wire and wire wrap one end of the wire to the end

to the top and bottom loops on the 3-strand side of the rhinestone connector instead of the bone circle.

16. Using 22-gauge wire, wire wrap one ½-inch (1.3 cm) piece of 3 mm cable chain to the center loop on the 3-strand side of the rhinestone connector. Thread one 12 mm sapphire gemstone bead on a head pin and wire wrap the head pin to the end of the cable chain. Thread one 5 mm sapphire bead on a head pin and wire wrap the head pin to the end of the cable chain. Wire wrap the charm to the end of the cable chain.

17. Using 22-gauge wire, make an "S" hook closure then wire wrap the hook through the single loop on the rhinestone connector.

of the 3 mm cable chain. Thread one 5 mm sapphire gemstone bead onto the wire, then wire wrap the end of the wire to a 2½-inch (6.3 cm) piece of 6 mm cable chain.

13. Using 24-gauge wire, wire wrap one 5 mm sapphire gemstone bead to the opposite end of the 6 mm chain. Wire wrap the opposite side of the bead to one ½-inch (1.3 cm) piece of 3 mm cable chain.

14. Using 22-gauge wire, wire wrap the end of the 3 mm cable chain to the bone circle.

15. Repeat steps 7 to 14 on the left side of the necklace, connecting the ends of each chain

Alternative Materials

You certainly don't have to go abroad in your search for vintage jewelry. Searches through local flea markets and thrift stores can turn up surprising, and affordable, treasures. There's no need to fret about finding pieces to use for this project. A glass, metal, or plastic ring can replace the bone circle, any locket will do, and a brooch can be used instead of the souvenir pin.

Sweet Bird That Carries My Heart Necklace

The bird pendant on this project was originally part of a religious art piece I found at a local flea market. The vintage rhinestone necklace was missing its centerpiece, but I couldn't pass it up. Once home, I added the bird as the centerpiece. The rustic look of the bird and the charm turn the sparkly rhinestone necklace into a piece that can be worn with anything from jeans and a T-shirt to a pretty black dress.

Instructions

1. Using the rotary drill, drill one hole at the tip of both sides of the bird's tail, about ¼ inch (0.6 cm) down from the tip.

2. Using a jump ring, attach the heart charm to the ring on the beak of the bird. Wire wrap the rhinestone dangle.

3. Wire wrap the tail of the bird to the necklace. This will serve as the pendant. Wire wrap the silver charm to the clasp.

Beads
- rhinestone dangle: 4 mm (10 inches [25.4 cm] long)

Findings & Found Objects
- bird pendant
- brass heart charm
- jump ring: 4 mm
- rhinestone necklace with clasp attached
- silver charm
- sterling silver wire: 22-gauge

Materials & Tools
- drill bit: ¼ inch (0.6 cm)
- pliers: flat-nose, round-nose
- rotary drill
- wire cutters

Pearls & Bird Locket Necklace

A very dear friend resides in France and she is always on the lookout for vintage baubles for me. The locket and little bird on this necklace were found on one of her treasure hunts. I found the vintage French paper featured in the locket in a trash can at a flea market in Paris. (Just goes to show how one man's trash is another man's treasure.)

Instructions

1. Cut a piece of decorative paper to fit inside the locket. Adhere the paper inside the locket with craft glue.

2. Glue the bird inside the locket using fast-drying jewelry cement; let dry.

3. Cut a piece of mica to fit inside the locket window. Place the mica over the bird and close the locket.

Beads

- baroque pearls: 10 x 15 mm (2)
- mercury glass tube beads: 3 x 20 mm (2)
- mother-of-pearl oblong beads: 5 x 10 mm (4)
- mother-of-pearl round beads: 5 mm (2); 8 mm (2)
- pink mother-of-pearl round beads: 8 mm (2); 12 mm (2)
- rhinestone disco ball beads: 10 mm (2)
- rhinestone rondelles: 6 mm (2)

Findings & Found Objects

- brass charm
- brass locket with window
- cable chain: 8 mm (1 inch [2.5 cm])
- cameo connector: 1-to-1 strand, 12 mm
- decorative paper
- mica sheet
- mother-of-pearl heart-shaped connectors: 1-to-1 strand, 14 mm (2)
- sterling silver wire: 22-gauge
- swivel hook

Materials & Tools

- craft glue
- drill bit: 1/16-inch (0.16 cm)
- fast-drying jewelry cement
- pliers: flat-nose, round-nose
- rotary drill
- scissors
- wire cutters

4. With a rotary drill, drill a hole at each of the top corners of the locket. *Note:* If your locket has a hole or ring at the center top edge, attach a 6 mm jump ring. Use the jump ring to attach the necklace and pendant as described below.

5. Wire wrap one mother-of-pearl oblong bead to the top right of the locket. Wire wrap the other side of the bead to the right side of one mother-of-pearl heart-shaped connector.

6. Cut a 4-inch (10.2 cm) piece of wire and wire wrap one end to the left side of the mother-of-pearl heart-shaped connector. In this order, thread the following onto the wire: baroque pearl, rhinestone rondelle, 5 mm mother-of-pearl bead. Make a wire-wrapped loop at the end of the wire.

7. Wire wrap one rhinestone disco ball bead to the wire-wrapped loop. Make a wire-wrapped loop at the opposite end of the bead.

8. Cut a 4-inch (10.2 cm) piece of wire and wire wrap one end to the disco ball bead. In this order, thread the following onto the wire: one 8 mm pink mother-of-pearl bead, one mercury glass tube bead, one 8 mm pink mother-of-pearl bead. Make a wire-wrapped loop at the end of the wire.

9. Wire wrap one 12 mm pink mother-of-pearl bead to the wire-wrapped loop. Make a wire-wrapped loop at the opposite end of the 12 mm pink mother-of-pearl bead. Wire wrap one oblong mother-of-pearl bead to the wire-wrapped loop. Make a wire-wrapped loop at the end of the wire.

10. Repeat steps 5 to 9 to complete the left side of the necklace.

11. On the right side of the necklace, wire wrap the oblong mother-of-pearl bead to the swivel hook.

12. On the left side of the necklace, wire wrap the oblong bead to the cameo connector.

13. Wire wrap the cable chain to the cameo connector, then wire wrap the charm to the end of the chain.

La Tour Eiffel Earrings

Beads
- rhinestone dangles: 4 mm (2)
- rhinestone disco ball beads: 3 mm (2)

Findings & Found Objects
- cable chain: 4 mm (two 1½-inch {3.8 cm} pieces); 6 mm (two ¼-inch [0.6 cm] pieces)
- charms: 16 mm (2)
- head pins (2)
- jump rings: 6 mm (4)
- sterling silver earring wires (2)

Materials & Tools
- pliers: flat-nose, round-nose
- wire cutters

When I found these matching Eiffel Tower charms, I knew they would be great to use in an earring project. I always consider the possibilities when shopping for small keepsakes, and when possible and affordable, I buy them in pairs.

Instructions

1. Using a jump ring, attach one rhinestone dangle and one connector to an Eiffel Tower charm.

2. Using a jump ring, attach the top of the connector to one ¼-inch (0.6 cm) piece of 6 mm cable chain.

3. Thread one disco ball bead onto a head pin, then wire wrap the head pin to one end of a 1½-inch (3.8 cm) piece of 4 mm cable chain.

4. Using flat-nose pliers, open the loop on one of the earring wires and slip the ends of both pieces of chain onto the loop; close the loop. Repeat steps 1 to 4 for second earring.

Heart Full of Memories Necklace

Beads
- crystal beads: 5 mm (2); 8 mm (2)
- freshwater pearls: 3 mm (8)
- rhinestone dangles: 5 mm (2)

Findings & Found Objects
- beading thread: silver
- cable chain: 8 mm (1 inch [2.5 cm])
- charm
- heart-shaped mother-of-pearl souvenir: 1½ x 1¾ inches (3.8 x 4.4 cm)
- jump rings: 4 mm (2)
- mother-of-pearl round-bead rosary chain (two 4½-inch [11.4 cm] pieces)
- rhinestone clasp: 4-to-4 strand, ¾ x 1½ inches (1.9 x 3.8 cm)
- rhinestone connectors: 5 x 20 mm (2)
- sterling silver wire

Materials & Tools
- pliers: flat-nose, round-nose
- sewing needle
- wire cutters

This mother-of-pearl and velvet heart souvenir was sent to me by a friend. The package was lost in the mail for nearly six months; just when I had given up hope of ever receiving it, a brown envelope appeared in my mailbox. The heart inside the package was more beautiful than I had imagined. A piece this unusual deserves to be the star of the show, so I chose subtle elements for the chain.

Instructions

1. Sew the rhinestone connectors to the top of the souvenir heart using the beading thread. Wire wrap one rhinestone dangle to the top edge of each rhinestone connector.

2. Wire wrap one 8 mm crystal bead to the rhinestone connector on the top right side of the heart, then wire wrap the opposite side of the bead to the end of

5. Cut a 5-inch (12.7 cm) piece of wire and wire wrap one end to the top left hole on the clasp. In this order, thread the following onto the wire: two freshwater pearls, the wire-wrapped loop at the end of the mother-of-pearl bead, two freshwater pearls. Wire wrap the end of the wire to the bottom left ring on the clasp.

6. Using a jump ring, attach one end of the cable chain to the middle ring on the left side of the clasp. Using a jump ring, attach the charm to the end of the chain.

one mother-of-pearl round-bead rosary chain. Wire wrap one 5 mm crystal bead to the opposite end of the chain, then make a wire-wrapped loop on the opposite side of the bead.

3. Repeat step 2 to complete the left side of the necklace.

4. Cut a 5-inch (12.7 cm) piece of wire and wire wrap one end to the top right hole on the clasp. Thread four freshwater pearls onto the wire, then wire wrap the end of the wire to the bottom right hole on the clasp.

Expert Advice

Turning Objects Into Pendants

When I received the heart shown on this necklace, it was not part of a pendant. Turning it into one was as easy as sewing the rhinestone connectors in place. There are a few ways to turn found objects into pendants, including soldering and wire wrapping. Instructions for these techniques can be found in beading guides and online.

Everyday Medal & Pearl Earrings

Beads
- mother-of-pearl beads: 6 mm (2)
- rhinestone dangles: 3 mm (2)

Findings & Found Objects
- head pins (2)
- souvenir medal charms: 20 mm (2)
- sterling silver earring hooks (2)
- sterling silver wire: 22-gauge

Materials & Tools
- pliers: flat-nose, round-nose
- wire cutters

These are my favorite earrings so I wear them often. They are lightweight and go with just about anything. The colors are muted, which I really like.

Instructions

1. Wire wrap one mother-of-pearl bead onto a head pin.

2. Cut one 3-inch (7.6 cm) piece of sterling silver wire. Thread one mother-of-pearl bead and one rhinestone dangle onto the wire, then wire wrap one end of the wire to the souvenir medal charm. *Note:* The mother-of-pearl bead and rhinestone dangles are inside the wire-wrapped loop.

3. Make a wire-wrapped loop at the opposite end of the wire. Using flat-nose pliers, open the loop on one earring wire, thread the wire-wrapped loop onto the earring wire loop, then close the loop. Repeat steps 1 to 3 for the second earring.

Souvenir Book Necklace

This tiny silver photo album locket is filled with miniature pictures of Paris monuments. In keeping with the theme of the pictures, a charm of the L' Arc de Triomphe dangles in front of the book. Notice how all of the chain pieces are different styles of cable chain.

Beads
- mercury glass bead: 20 mm
- mother-of-pearl beads: 6 mm (3); 10 mm (2)
- ruby gemstone beads: 3 mm (12); 20 mm (1)
- sapphire gemstone oblong beads: 4 x 10 mm (2)

Findings & Found Objects
- cable chain: 6 mm (2½-inch [6.4 cm] piece); 8 mm (one ¼-inch [0.6 cm] piece and two 1-inch [2.5 cm] pieces)
- charm
- jump rings: 4 mm (1); 12 mm (1)
- long and short cable chain: 12 mm (3½ inches [8.9 cm])

- metal photo album locket: 1 x 1½ inches (2.5 x 3.8 cm)
- rhinestone clasp: 2-to-2 strand
- rhinestone necklace piece (2 inches [5.1 cm])
- rosary bead chain (1½ inches [3.8 cm])
- spring ring: 18 mm
- sterling silver wire: 24-gauge

Materials & Tools
- pliers: flat-nose, round-nose
- wire cutters

Instructions

Connect the ring on the souvenir book to the 14 mm jump ring, then connect the jump ring to the 18 mm spring ring. Wire wrap the charm to the 14 mm jump ring, making sure the charm shows at the front of the metal photo album locket.

To make the left side of the necklace:

1. Using flat-nose pliers, open the 18 mm spring ring and attach it to the ¼-inch (0.6 cm) piece of 8 mm cable chain; close the ring. Open the ring on the bottom of the rhinestone necklace piece and connect it to the end of the cable chain piece; close the ring.

2. Wire wrap one sapphire gemstone bead to the top right side of the rhinestone chain piece, then wire wrap the opposite side of the bead to a rhinestone connector.

3. Wire wrap one 10 mm mother-of-pearl bead to the top of the rhinestone connector, then wire wrap the opposite side of the mother-of-pearl bead to one end of a 2½-inch (6.4 cm) piece of 6 mm cable chain. Wire wrap one 6 mm mother-of-pearl bead to the opposite end of the chain. Make a wire-wrapped loop at the opposite side of the mother-of-pearl bead.

4. Wire wrap one sapphire gemstone bead to the top left side of the rhinestone chain piece, then wire wrap the opposite side of the bead to a rhinestone connector.

5. Wire wrap one 10 mm mother-of-pearl bead to the top of the rhinestone connector, then wire wrap the opposite side of the mother-of-pearl bead to one end of a 2½-inch (6.4 cm) piece of 6 mm cable chain. Wire wrap one 6 mm mother-of-pearl bead to the opposite end of the chain. Make a wire-wrapped loop at the opposite side of the mother-of-pearl bead.

To make the right side of the necklace:

1. Wire wrap the 20 mm ruby gemstone bead to the 18 mm connector ring, then wire wrap the opposite end of the ruby gemstone bead to the 3½-inch (8.9 cm) piece of 12 mm cable chain. Wire wrap the mercury glass bead to the opposite end of the chain. Make a wire-wrapped loop at the opposite end of the mercury glass bead.

Alternative Materials

Vintage photo album lockets aren't easy to find, but an Internet search for "photo album charm" or "book pendant" will provide a few options. If you like the look of this necklace but are unable to find a similar locket, consider using a new photo locket instead. To achieve a vintage look, oxidize the locket. Insert desired photos after oxidizing the piece.

2. Wire wrap the rosary bead chain to the wire-wrapped loop at the end of the mercury bead. Wire wrap one 6 mm mother-of-pearl bead to the end of the rosary bead chain. Make a wire-wrapped loop on the opposite end of the mother-of-pearl bead.

To connect the necklace to the clasp:

1. Cut one 5-inch (12.7 cm) piece of wire and wire wrap one end to the top right ring on the rhinestone clasp. In this order, thread the following onto the wire: three 3 mm ruby gemstone beads, the wire-wrapped loop at the end of the right side chain, three

3 mm ruby gemstone beads. Wire wrap the end of the wire to the bottom right ring on the clasp.

2. Cut one 5-inch (12.7 cm) piece of wire and wire wrap one end to the top left ring on the rhinestone clasp. In this order, thread the following onto the wire: one 3 mm ruby gemstone bead, the loop at the end of the chain on the left side of the connector, four 3 mm ruby gemstone beads, the loop at the end of the chain on the right side of the connector, and one 3 mm ruby gemstone bead. Wire wrap the end of the wire to the bottom left ring on the clasp.

Expert Advice

Connection Solutions
Because these projects were made with vintage pieces, the findings and other elements you use will be different from those shown here. If the ends of your pieces don't open, use a jump ring to connect them. If your rhinestone necklace or clasp has only a single point of connection, attach the beginning of the right and left sides of the necklace at that single point of connection.

Chapter 4

French Inspirations

Oh, for the love of France. I do have French ancestry, but if I ever lived another life, I know it must have been in the heart of Paris in the early 18th century, when artists of all types were hanging out at chic cafés in abundance and inspiration was everywhere. Such is the depth of my adoration for France.

In this chapter I share with you my love for Paris and its people. Three historical figures find their way into these projects time and again; Marie Antoinette, the young queen who had a fondness for beautiful things; brave, young Joan of Arc, who had such a strong sense of loyalty to her beliefs; and Napoleon Bonaparte, the French emperor.

When using Marie Antoinette as my inspiration, I felt a need to keep the piece soft and feminine; when working on a piece with Joan's image, I wanted the look to be strong and sturdy; and when working on a Napoleon-themed piece, I tried to make it a bit masculine with a military influence.

The bracelets, earrings, and necklaces found in this chapter were created from a variety of objects that I find are not only beautiful, but help preserve a little bit of history.

I have put to use old brooches and forgotten charms and lovingly pieced together disregarded rhinestone parts. I have also mixed leather with medals and buttons, and blended pearls with chunky beads. Watch fobs and assorted chains are embellished with one-of-a-kind pendants and other funky finds.

When choosing elements to use in your projects, consider blending items that convey the meaning of each piece of jewelry or the person who inspired it. Your finished pieces will tell their stories for generations to come.

Portrait of Marie Necklace

Hand-painted portrait pendants are hard to come by, so I snatched this one up. This Marie Antoinette portrait shows how she might have looked while on one of her visits to her country estate: relaxed and beautiful. This is a great project on which to use mismatched or orphaned rhinestone connectors.

Instructions

To make the pieced necklace:

1. Using flat-nose pliers, open the ring on the pendant and connect it to the ring at the bottom of the rhinestone necklace centerpiece. *Note:* If you can't open the ring, wire wrap the pendant to the ring instead.

2. Using jump rings, attach one rhinestone connector to the left side of the rhinestone necklace centerpiece. Attach four rhinestone connectors together.

3. Wire wrap one ruby gemstone bead to the end of the last rhinestone connector, then wire wrap the opposite end of the ruby gemstone bead to one 2½-inch (6.4 cm) piece of decorative chain. Using a jump ring, attach the end of the necklace to the right

Beads
- ruby gemstone beads: 12 mm (2)

Findings & Found Objects
- crystal chain (21-inch [53.3 cm] length)
- decorative chain (two 2½-inch [6.4 cm] pieces)
- jump rings: 5 mm (16)
- mother-of-pearl round-bead rosary chain (1 inch [2.5 cm] piece)
- rhinestone clasp: 1-to-1 strand, 5 x 15 mm
- rhinestone connectors: 1-to-1 strand, various styles and sizes (4)
- rhinestone necklace centerpiece with connector for pendant

Materials & Tools
- pliers: flat-nose, round-nose
- wire cutters

side of the clasp. Repeat steps 2 and 3 on the left side of the necklace.

To attach the crystal chain and finish the necklace:

1. Wire wrap the ends of the chain to the jump rings on the sides of the clasp.

2. Using jump rings, attach the rosary bead chain to the right side of the clasp, then attach the charm to the end of the rosary bead chain.

Sassy Girl Wears Pink Necklace

Beads
- baroque pearls: 10 mm (2)
- mother-of-pearl oblong beads: 5 x 10 mm (2)
- mother-of-pearl round beads: 5 mm (8)

Findings & Found Objects
- cable chain: 6 mm (2 inches [5.1 cm])
- charms (2)
- decorative paper
- jump rings: 6 mm (2)
- marquisette pendant or round connector: 50 mm
- mica
- pink crystal chain: 7 mm (two 6-inch [15.2 cm] pieces)
- portrait button: 25 mm
- rhinestone clasp
- sterling silver wire: 22-gauge, 24-gauge
- velvet ribbon

Materials & Tools
- jewelry cement
- pliers: flat-nose, round-nose
- scissors
- wire cutters

Marie Antoinette's attention to detail has drawn admirers to her acute sense of style for centuries. No one else has made feathers and the colors pink and baby blue look so good.

Instructions

1. Using jewelry cement, glue the portrait button to the center of the marquisette piece; let dry.

2. Using 22-gauge wire, wire wrap the end of one 6-inch (15.2 cm) piece of pink crystal chain to the top right side of the marquisette piece. Using 24-gauge wire, wire wrap one baroque pearl to the opposite end of the chain. Make a wire-wrapped loop on the opposite side of the baroque pearl.

3. Using 24-gauge wire, wire wrap one mother-of-pearl oblong bead to the wire-wrapped loop. Make a wire-wrapped loop on the opposite side of the mother-of-pearl oblong bead.

6. Using jump rings, attach the cable chain to the bottom right ring of the clasp then attach the charm to the bottom of the chain.

7. Turn the pendant face down. Cut a piece of decorative paper to fit the center of the back of the pendant, then glue the paper in place. Glue the charm onto the paper.

8. Cut a piece of mica the same size as the paper. Place glue around the edges of the paper and adhere mica piece to the paper. Cut a piece of ribbon to fit around the edges of the mica then glue the ribbon in place.

4. Cut one 5-inch (12.7 cm) piece of 24-gauge wire. Wire wrap one end of the wire to the top right ring on the rhinestone clasp. In this order, thread the following onto the wire: two round mother-of-pearl beads, the wire-wrapped loop on the end of the chain, two round mother-of-pearl beads. Wire wrap the end of the wire to the bottom right ring on the clasp.

5. Repeat steps 2 to 4 to make the left side of the necklace.

Alternative Materials

You can blend all types of things to make the centerpiece. Use what you like so you will create something that reflects your personal style. Once I used old identification badges mixed with ruby gemstone beads to create a stunning centerpiece and I loved the results—fun without the frills.

Rhinestones & Medals Earrings

Beads
- rhinestone dangles: 5 mm (6)

Findings & Found Objects
- medal charms
- rhinestone connectors: 1-to-1 strand (2)
- sterling silver earring wires (2)
- sterling silver wire: 22-gauge

Materials & Tools
- pliers: flat-nose, round-nose
- wire cutters

I found these great medal charms in France as well. Mixing the medal with rhinestones takes these earrings from plain to dazzling.

Instructions

1. Cut one 3-inch (7.6 cm) piece of wire and wire wrap one end to the top of a charm. Thread three rhinestone dangles onto the wire then wire wrap the end of the wire to the bottom ring on one rhinestone connector.

2. Using flat-nose pliers, open the loop on one earring wire, thread the top ring of the connector onto the loop, then close the loop.

3. Repeat steps 1 and 2 to complete the second earring.

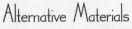

Alternative Materials

If you have difficulty finding rhinestone connectors, use links from a rhinestone bracelet or necklace. Any small bead could be used in place of the dangles.

Heir of France Necklace

Findings & Found Objects
- mosaic connectors: 1-to-1 strand (2)
- portrait brooch with filigree work around edges
- sterling silver wire: 24-gauge
- various rhinestone bracelet pieces with connectors attached (two 7-inch [17.8 cm] pieces)

Materials & Tools
- pliers: flat-nose, round-nose
- wire cutters

I collect vintage rhinestone bracelets and necklaces and use portions of them on many of the pieces of jewelry I create. This necklace was made with elements from six different rhinestone pieces.

Instructions

1. Using flat-nose pliers, open one side of a rhinestone connector and attach it to the top right side of the brooch, then close the connector.

2. Using the same technique, attach the mosaic connector to the rhinestone connector.

3. Continue attaching rhinestone connectors until there is a 7-inch (17.8 cm) chain.

4. Wire wrap one side of the clasp to the end of the chain. *Note:* Attach more connectors if you desire a longer necklace.

5. Repeat steps 1 and 4 to complete the left side of the necklace.

Joan's Pocketbook Necklace

The pocketbook-shaped Joan of Arc locket featured on this necklace is one of the most unusual pieces I have found. Because it's a bit bulky, I used chunky chain pieces to create the necklace. The ornate chain and mother-of-pearl bead element is actually a watch fob. The chunky chain is from an old identification bracelet. Notice how the clasp is at the front of the necklace.

Beads
- mother-of-pearl oblong beads: 10 mm (2); 13 mm (1)

Findings & Found Objects
- book locket
- cable chain: 4 mm (three ½-inch [1.3 cm] pieces); 6 mm (1-inch [2.5 cm] piece)
- charm
- decorative watch fob (4 inches [10.2 cm])
- identification bracelet chain (7 inches [17.8 cm])
- jump rings: 5 mm (3); 8 mm (1)
- mother-of-pearl heart-shaped connector: 2-to-1 strand
- spring ring: 20 mm
- sterling silver wire: 22-gauge, 24-gauge
- swivel hook clasp: 20 mm

Materials & Tools
- pliers: flat-nose, round-nose
- wire cutters

Instructions

1. Using the 8 mm jump ring, attach the book locket to the spring ring.

2. Using 22-gauge wire, wire wrap one end of the identification bracelet chain to the loop on top of the spring ring.

3. Using 24-gauge wire, wire wrap one end of the 6 mm cable chain to the end of the identification bracelet chain. Wire wrap the charm to the opposite end of the cable chain.

4. Using 24-gauge wire, wire wrap the 10 mm mother-of-pearl oblong bead to the end of the identification bracelet chain, then wire wrap the opposite end of the mother-of-pearl oblong bead to the end of a ½-inch (1.3 cm) piece of 4 mm cable chain. Using a 5 mm jump ring, attach the opposite end of the cable chain to the bottom of the mother-of-pearl heart-shaped connector.

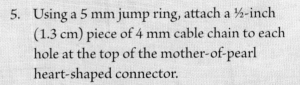

Alternative Materials

If you have difficulty finding decorative watch fobs, feel free to use lengths of pretty bracelets or necklaces instead. There are no hard-and-fast rules to follow when creating rejuvenated jewels. Also, instead of using the swivel clasp on this necklace, try an "S"-hook closure. If you can't find a vintage version you like, simply make your own.

5. Using a 5 mm jump ring, attach a ½-inch (1.3 cm) piece of 4 mm cable chain to each hole at the top of the mother-of-pearl heart-shaped connector.

6. Wire wrap one 10 mm mother-of-pearl bead to the end of each chain, then wire wrap the opposite end of each bead to one end of the decorative watch fob.

7. Using a 5 mm jump ring, attach the opposite end of the decorative watch fob to the end of the swivel hook clasp.

Expert Advice

Wire Connections Made

Though it may be tempting to use whatever gauge wire you have on hand, always consider the weight of the elements when making your necklace. The chunky pieces require a stronger wire—24-gauge at least. When attaching clasps and closures to heavier chains, use 22-gauge wire. Your finished pieces will hold up for years to come.

Napoleon on Leather Necklace

Do you have any old military ribbons in your drawers of family memorabilia? This necklace provides a fabulous way to show them off. Ribbon, leather, rhinestones, and metal are mixed together in this interesting piece.

Instructions

1. Thread the sapphire gemstone bead onto a head pin then wire wrap the head pin to the clasp on the book locket.

2. Using metal thread, sew the ring at the top of the book locket to the bottom middle edge of the military ribbon.

3. Wire wrap one rhinestone bracelet piece to the right side of the bar that holds the military ribbon.

Beads
- sapphire gemstone beads: 5 mm (2)

Findings & Found Objects
- book locket
- cable chain: 6 mm (two ½-inch [1.3 cm] pieces)
- charm
- end cap connectors: 10 mm (2)
- head pins (3)
- jump rings: 6 mm (4)
- leather ribbon: ½ inch (1.3 cm) wide (two 17-inch [43.2 cm] lengths)
- metal buttons with shanks: 14 mm (2)
- metal thread
- military ribbon on a bar
- needle
- rhinestone bracelet pieces (two 1½-inch [3.2 cm] pieces)
- sterling silver wire: 22-gauge
- swivel clasps: 20 mm (2)

Materials & Tools
- awl
- fast-drying jewelry cement
- pliers: flat-nose, round-nose
- scissors

4. Thread the swivel clasp on the end of the rhinestone bracelet piece.

5. Using a jump ring, attach one end of a ½-inch (1.3 cm) piece of cable chain to the bottom of the swivel clasp.

6. Using fast-drying jewelry cement, glue one end of a 17-inch (43.2 cm) piece of leather ribbon inside one end cap connector, making sure the leather side faces out. Let the cement dry.

7. Using a jump ring, attach the end of the ½-inch (1.3 cm) piece of cable chain to the end cap connector.

8. Using the awl, pierce a hole near the center bottom edge of the leather ribbon.

9. Thread one sapphire gemstone bead onto a head pin, poke the top of the head pin through the hole in the ribbon, then wire wrap the shank of one metal button onto the end of the head pin.

10. Repeat steps 3 to 9 on the left side.

11. Wire wrap the charm to the shank on one of the metal buttons.

Charming Bracelet

Findings & Found Objects
- charms (5)
- jump rings: 5 mm (5); 6 mm (1)
- lobster claw clasp
- watch fob chain (7 inches [17.8 cm])

Materials & Tools
- pliers: flat-nose, round-nose
- wire cutters

This incredibly easy project was made with a handful of French-themed charms and an old watch fob. The finished bracelet is a wonderful example of how great pieces of jewelry do not need to be hard to make.

Instructions

1. Using 5 mm jump rings, attach the charms to the watch fob chain where desired.

2. Using the 6 mm jump ring, attach the lobster claw clasp to one end of the watch fob chain.

Alternative Materials

If you have a hard time finding an old watch fob, an identification bracelet can be used instead. Silver link bracelets also work well for this project and are easy to find in bead and craft stores. To give an aged appearance to shiny new pieces, simply oxidize them.

Memories of France Necklace

Made with a rare Joan of Arc pin, rosary pieces, and a book locket, this necklace was created to honor a member of my family. A tintype of this distant relative is hidden on the back of the decorative pin. The carved bead, connectors, and mother-of-pearl chain were part of an old rosary. I love the beauty and history of these pieces. Every part blends to create a necklace that is chunky but feminine.

Beads

- freshwater pearls: various sizes and colors (6-8)
- mercury glass beads: 3 mm (2); 12 mm (1)
- rhinestone dangles: 3 mm (2)

Findings & Found Objects

- book locket
- cable chain: 5 mm (1 inch [2.5 cm])
- charm
- decorative paper
- decorative pin
- ivory triangle connector: 18 mm
- jump rings: 5 mm (6)
- mother-of-pearl heart-shaped connector: 2-to-1 strand, 12 mm
- mother-of-pearl square-bead rosary chain: 7 mm (four 2-inch [5.1 cm] pieces)

- rhinestone clasp: 3-to-3 strand, 10 x 20 mm
- rosary bead chain (2 links)
- round metal pendant: 30 mm
- sterling silver wire: 24-gauge
- tintype

Materials & Tools

- drill bit: ¼ inch (0.6 cm)
- fast-drying jewelry cement
- jewelry file
- pencil
- pliers: flat-nose, round-nose
- rotary drill
- scissors
- wire cutters

Instructions

1. Using wire cutters, remove the pin back from the decorative pin. Smooth any rough edges using the jewelry file.

2. Trace around the round pendant on decorative paper then cut out the shape. Adhere the paper to the back of the round pendant using fast-drying jewelry cement.

3. Using the rotary drill, drill three holes in the round pendant as follows: one on the right side, one on the left side, one at the bottom center. Each hole should be ¼ inch (0.6 cm) in from the edge of the pendant.

4. Wire wrap the book locket to the bottom center hole on the round pendant. Wire wrap one freshwater pearl to the hole on the right side of the round pendant. Make a wire-wrapped loop on the opposite side of the freshwater pearl.

5. Wire wrap a freshwater pearl to the wire-wrapped loop. Make a wire-wrapped loop on the opposite side of the freshwater pearl.

6. Wire wrap the 12 mm mercury glass bead to the wire-wrapped loop. Make a wire-wrapped loop on the opposite side of the mercury glass bead.

7. Wire wrap the bottom ring of the mother-of-pearl heart-shaped connector to the wire-wrapped loop.

8. Wire wrap a 1-inch (2.5 cm) piece of cable chain to the top right ring of the heart-shaped connector. Using a jump ring, attach the end of the cable chain to one end of a 2-inch (5.1 cm) piece of mother-of-pearl square-bead rosary chain. Using a jump ring, attach the end of the mother-of-pearl square-bead rosary chain to the top right ring on the clasp.

9. Repeat step 8 on the top left side of the mother-of-pearl heart-shaped connector, but this time, attach the end of the mother-of-pearl square-bead rosary chain to the bottom right ring on the clasp.

wire then wire wrap the other end of the wire to the end of one 2-inch (5.1 cm) piece of mother-of-pearl square-bead rosary chain. Using a jump ring, attach the opposite end of the mother-of-pearl square-bead rosary chain to the top left ring on the clasp.

14. Repeat step 13 on the top left side of the decorative pin, but this time, attach the end connector of the mother-of-pearl square-bead rosary chain to the bottom left ring on the clasp.

15. Using jump rings, attach one end of the cable chain to the center of the left side of the clasp, then attach the charm to the bottom of the chain.

16. Trim the tintype to fit on the back of the decorative pin, then adhere it using fast-drying jewelry cement; let dry.

10. Wire wrap one freshwater pearl through the hole on the left side of the pendant. Wire wrap the opposite side of the freshwater pearl to the bottom loop of the rosary bead chain link.

11. Wire wrap the bottom of the ivory triangle connector to the top of the rosary bead link.

12. Wire wrap one freshwater pearl to the top of each side of the triangle-shaped ivory connector, then wire wrap the freshwater pearls to the bottom of the decorative pin.

13. Cut one 3-inch (7.6 cm) piece of wire and wire wrap one end to the top right side of the pin. Thread one 3 mm mercury glass bead and one rhinestone dangle onto the

Expert Advice

Honoring History

When creating memory jewelry, consider using items that were special to someone in your family. Elements such as athletic or military medals could be used along with wedding, anniversary, or work-related items. Not only does the finished piece honor your loved one, the memories recalled make creating the piece a special experience.

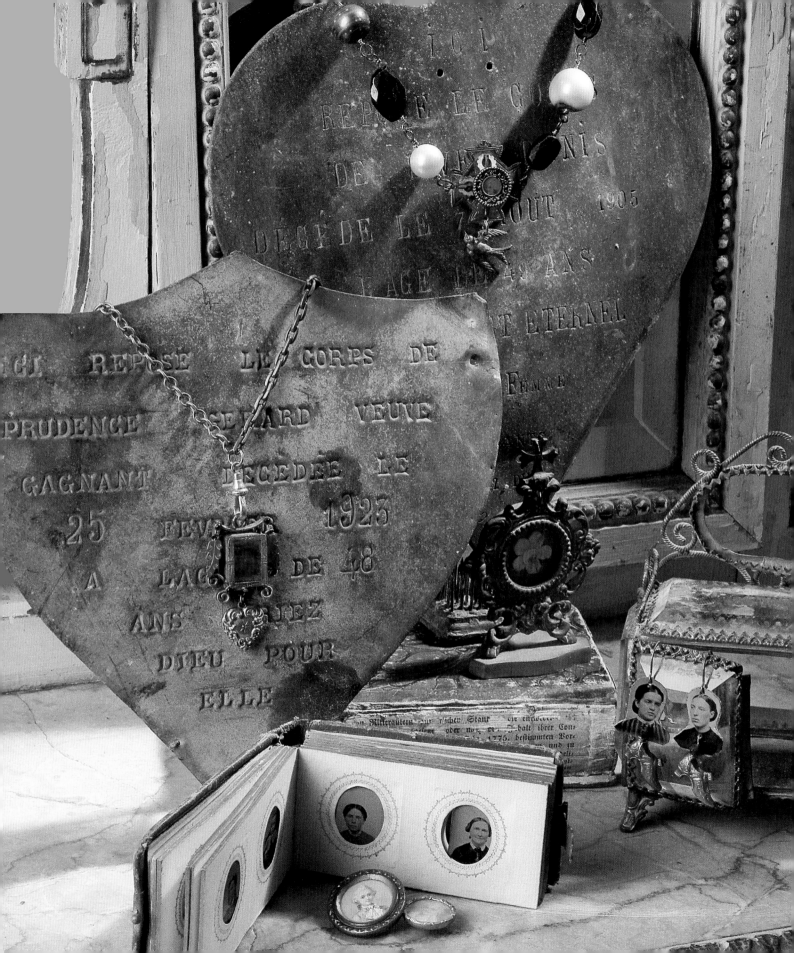

Pictures of the Past

There is something so special about old tintypes. They capture moments from the past and are reminders of a simpler time. A tintype is a photograph made on a thin piece of darkened iron. Because there was no negative from which duplicate prints could be made, the images were truly unique. Tintypes were popular from the mid-1800s to the early 1900s, most likely because they were light-weight, durable, and inexpensive to produce.

I often use very small tintypes that are also known as gemtypes. Gemtypes measure no larger than 1-inch (2.5 cm) square and al-most exclusively feature portraits. Individual tintypes abound at flea markets and antique stores. Gemtypes are most often found in miniature photo albums. I can sit for hours looking through old albums, wondering about the stories behind the images. There are myriad ways to include images in your jewelry. They can be hidden in or behind lockets and pendants, attached to bracelets, and dangled from earrings.

The projects in the chapter all incorporate vintage images. The sepia tones of the images mix well with the timeworn patinas of vintage metals and the rich colors of gemstone beads used in the projects. In one project a military ribbon bracelet is adorned with an image of a wartime wife. One necklace features a locket that holds a portrait button inside and a gem-type on the back, while another was made with unique pearls, chunky gemstone beads, and an embellished medal.

Sweet Sister Necklace

The image used on this necklace reminds me of the special relationship shared by my twin daughters. I used very simple pieces when creating this necklace. The finished piece is a great example of less is more.

Instructions

1. Using the awl, make a hole at the top and bottom of the tintype, ¼ inch (0.6 cm) in from the edge.

2. Cut one 5-inch (12.7 cm) piece of wire. Thread the ends of the wire through the bottom holes on the round glass connector then through the back of the hole on the bottom of the tintype. (The ends of the wire should now be in the front of the tintype.) Wire wrap the ruby gemstone teardrop bead to the ends of the wire.

3. Repeat step 2 at the top of the glass connector, but this time, wire wrap five rhinestone dangles to each end of the wire. Wire wrap the bottom of the silver connector to one of the rhinestone dangles. Wire wrap the top right ring on the connector to the end of one piece of cable chain.

4. Cut one 5-inch piece of 24-gauge wire and wire wrap one of the wires to the opposite end of the cable chain. In this order, thread the following onto the wire: 3 mm glass bead, glass long bicone bead, 3 mm glass bead. Wire wrap the end of the wire to the top right ring on the rhinestone clasp.

Beads
- glass beads: 3 mm (8)
- glass long bicone beads: 3 x 10 mm (4)
- rhinestone dangles: 4 mm (5)
- ruby gemstone teardrop bead: 8 mm

Findings & Found Objects
- cable chain: 10 mm (two 7½-inch [19.1 cm] pieces)
- rhinestone clasp: 10 x 25 mm
- round glass connector with two holes
- silver connector: 2-to-1 strand, 8 mm
- sterling silver wire: 24-gauge, 26-gauge
- tintype

Materials & Tools
- awl
- pliers: flat-nose, round-nose
- wire cutters

5. Repeat step 4, but this time, wire wrap the end of the wire to the bottom right ring on the clasp.

6. Repeat steps 4 and 5 to complete the left side of the necklace.

Hollis & Her Watch Fob Necklace

Beads
- flat-backed rhinestones: 3 mm (3)
- ruby gemstone beads: 3 mm (3)

Findings & Found Objects
- cable chain (one 6½-inch [16.5 cm] piece; one 9½-inch [24.2 cm] piece)
- clock charm
- decorative paper
- heart charm
- jump rings: 6 mm (5)
- lobster claw clasps: 15 mm (1); 20 mm (1)
- locket with window front
- mica sheet
- portrait button
- silver charm
- tintype
- toggle bar

Materials & Tools
- fast-drying jewelry cement
- pliers: flat-nose, round-nose
- scissors
- wire cutters

When I found this locket it was empty and missing its back piece. Even so, I couldn't wait to use it. I put a tiny portrait button and rhinestones inside and used a tintype to close the back of the locket.

Instructions

1. Trim the tintype to fit the back of the locket. Cut a piece of decorative paper the same size and shape of the tintype. Adhere the paper to the back of the tintype with fast-drying jewelry cement.

2. Cut a piece of mica to fit inside the locket. Add fast-drying jewelry cement around the front edges of the mica then adhere the mica to the inside front edges of the locket.

3. Place the portrait button, flat-backed rhinestones, and ruby gemstone beads inside the locket pendant. Add fast-drying jewelry cement around the edges of the decorative paper and adhere paper to the back edges of the locket.

4. Using a jump ring, attach the heart charm to the bottom of the locket. Thread the top ring on the locket onto the 20 mm lobster claw clasp.

5. Using a jump ring, attach one end of both pieces of chain to the bottom of the 20 mm lobster claw clasp.

6. Using a jump ring, attach the bottom of the 15 mm lobster claw clasp to the end of the 6½-inch (16.5 cm) piece of cable chain.

7. Using a jump ring, attach the clock charm and the silver charm to the end of the 9½-inch (24.2 cm) piece of cable chain.

8. Using a jump ring, attach the toggle bar to the end of the 9½-inch (24.2 cm) piece of cable chain. Attach the lobster claw clasp to the toggle bar.

Girls Love Their Shoes Earrings

These fun earrings provide a simple way to display old family photographs. When trimming the pictures, make sure to leave room at the top and bottom to accommodate the holes.

Instructions

1. Trim one tintype to desired shape. Using the awl, make a hole on top and bottom of the tintype.

2. Cut one 4-inch (10.2 cm) piece of wire and wire wrap one end to the shoe charm. Thread one garnet gemstone bead onto the wire, then wire wrap the end of the wire through the hole on the bottom of the tintype.

3. Using flat-nose pliers, open the loop on one earring hook, thread the top of the tintype onto the loop, then close the loop.

4. Repeat steps 1 to 3 to make the second earring.

Beads
- garnet gemstone beads: 3 mm (2)

Findings & Found Objects
- shoe charms (2)
- sterling silver earring wires (2)
- sterling silver wire: 24-gauge
- tintypes: approximately 15 mm (2)

Materials & Tools
- awl
- pliers: flat-nose, round-nose
- scissors
- wire cutters

Expert Advice
Preserving Photos
To protect the surface of the pictures, consider spraying them with a sealer or covering them with embossing enamel. Always follow manufacturer's directions.

Military Ribbon Bracelet

The military ribbon shown here has an engraved medal stating the name of the honoree and the year 1923. I added a lovely vintage photograph and connected the piece using a vintage rhinestone clasp.

Instructions

1. Using the awl, make one hole in each corner of the tintype ¼ inch (0.6 cm) in from the edge of the tintype.

2. Place one brad through each hole and then through the ribbon on the ½ x 2-inch (1.3 x 5.1 cm) military ribbon. Open the brads to secure them to the ribbon.

3. Attach the flat-backed rhinestone bead to the center of the 1 x 3½-inch (2.5 x 8.9 cm) military ribbon using jewelry cement.

4. Using the rotary drill, drill two holes at the edge of the 1 x 3½-inch (2.5 x 8.9 cm) military ribbon next to the tintype. Wire wrap one end of the 2-inch (5.1 cm) piece of cable chain through one hole then thread the

Beads
- flat-backed square rhinestone bead: 12 mm

Findings & Found Objects
- cable chain: 3 mm (two ½-inch [1.3 cm] pieces; two ¼-inch [0.6 cm] pieces); 7 mm (one 2-inch [5.1 cm] piece)
- charm
- jump rings: 6 mm (5)
- metal brads: 4 mm (4)
- military ribbons (one 1 x 3½-inch [2.5 x 8.9 cm] piece; one ½ x 2-inch [1.3 x 5.1 cm] piece)
- rhinestone clasp: 5 x 20 mm
- sterling silver wire: 26-gauge
- tintype
- tube connector: 10 x 15 mm

Materials & Tools
- awl
- drill bit: ¹⁄₁₆-inch (0.16 cm)
- fast-drying jewelry cement
- pliers: flat-nose, round-nose
- rotary drill
- wire cutters

chain through the tube connector. Wire wrap the end of the chain through the opposite hole.

5. Using a jump ring, attach the ring on the tube connector to one end of the rhinestone clasp.

6. Using jump rings, attach one ½-inch (1.3 cm) piece of cable chain to each ring at the top edge of the 1 x 3½-inch (2.5 x 8.9 cm) military ribbon, then attach the opposite ends of both chains to another jump ring. Attach two ¼-inch (0.6 cm) pieces of cable chain to the same jump ring. Attach the ends of the chains to the rings on the end of the ½ x 2-inch (1.3 x 5.1 cm) military ribbon. Wire wrap the charm to the center jump ring.

7. Attach the connector on the remaining side of the clasp to the end of the ½ x 2-inch (1.3 x 5.1 cm) military ribbon.

Alternative Materials

If you have difficulty finding military ribbons to use in this project, consider using strips of leather instead. Attach end caps with loops to the edges of the leather strips and use pieces of chain to connect the leather pieces. Leather supplies can be found at craft and hobby stores.

Tin Man Earrings

Beads
- garnet gemstone beads: 3 mm (2)
- rhinestone dangles: 3 mm (2)

Findings & Found Objects
- decorative paper
- silver oval ring connectors:
  7 mm (2)
- sterling silver earring hooks (2)
- sterling silver wire: 24-gauge
- tintypes (2)

Materials & Tools
- awl
- craft glue
- pliers: flat-nose, round-nose
- scissors
- wire cutters

These earrings are a simplified version of the Girls Love Their Shoes Earrings (see page 91). You can also make this project using small images of favorite places or things. If you use color photographs, coordinate the bead colors with colors in the images.

Instructions

1. Trim one tintype to desired shape. Trace the tintype onto the decorative paper and cut out. Using craft glue, adhere the decorative paper to the back of the tintype. Let the glue dry.

2. Using the awl, make a hole at the top of the tintype ¼6 inch (0.6 cm) in from the top edge.

3. Cut one 4-inch (10.2 cm) piece of wire, thread one rhinestone dangle onto the end of the wire, and make a wire-wrapped loop. Thread one garnet gemstone bead onto the wire, then wire wrap the end of the wire to the silver oval ring connector.

4. Using flat-nose pliers, open the ring on one earring wire. Thread the silver oval connector onto the loop then close the loop.

5. Repeat steps 1 to 4 to make the second earring.

Jon Jon's Necklace

This necklace is named for the sweet man who sold me the beautiful pearls on it. I have purchased pearls from him a few times over the years, and am always amazed at his gorgeous selections. The day I bought these pricey saltwater pearls, we talked for hours—it took that long to talk me into spending the money. But I knew I would regret passing up these natural beauties if I didn't buy them.

Beads

- crystal beads: 5 mm (2)
- garnet gemstone beads: various sizes and colors (3)
- large saltwater pearls: various sizes and colors (3)
- mother-of-pearl bead: 5 mm
- sapphire gemstone bead: 15 mm

Findings & Found Objects

- bird charm
- decorative pin: 25 x 25 mm
- flower pin with three holes
- jump rings: 5 mm (1); 7 mm (1)
- metal heart-shaped connector: 2-to-1 strand, 12 mm
- mother-of-pearl heart-shaped connector: 2-to-1 strand, 8 mm
- mother-of-pearl round-bead rosary chain: 5 mm (two 2-inch [5.1 cm] pieces)
- portrait button: 12 mm
- rhinestone heart-shaped pendant
- silver charm
- silver rosary bead chain: 5 mm (two 1-inch [2.5 cm] pieces)
- sterling silver wire: 24-gauge
- tintype

Materials & Tools

- drill bit: 3/64 inch (0.5 cm)
- fast-drying jewelry cement
- jewelry file
- pliers: flat-nose, round-nose
- rotary drill
- scissors
- wire cutters

 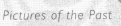

jewelry cement. Using a 7 mm jump ring, attach the bird charm to the bottom of the decorative pin.

5. Wire wrap one saltwater pearl to the hole on the right side of the decorative pin, then make a wire-wrapped loop on the opposite side of the saltwater pearl.

6. Wire wrap one garnet gemstone bead to the wire-wrapped loop, then make a wire-wrapped loop on the opposite side of the garnet gemstone bead.

7. Wire wrap one saltwater pearl to the wire-wrapped loop. Make a wire-wrapped loop on the opposite end of the saltwater pearl.

Instructions

1. Remove the backs from both pins using wire cutters. Smooth rough edges using jewelry file.

2. Using the rotary drill, drill three holes in the decorative pin: one on the right side, one on the left side, and one on the bottom.

3. Adhere the portrait button to the front of the decorative pin using fast-drying jewelry cement.

4. Trim the tintype to fit on the back of the decorative pin and adhere it using fast-drying

Alternative Materials

If you prefer to not use a drill, replace the decorative pendant with a pendant or locket that has filigree edges. You can connect wire-wrapped loops or jumps rings directly to the filigree edges. Complete the necklace as directed.

8. Wire wrap one garnet gemstone bead to the wire-wrapped loop, then wire wrap the opposite end of the garnet gemstone bead to the bottom of the metal heart-shaped connector.

9. Wire wrap a 1-inch (2.5 cm) piece of silver rosary bead chain to each ring at the top of the metal heart-shaped rosary bead connector. Wire wrap one mother-of-pearl bead to the end of each silver rosary bead chain, then wire wrap the opposite end of each mother-of-pearl bead to the rhinestone heart-shaped pendant.

10. Using a 5 mm jump ring, attach the hook to the rhinestone heart-shaped connector. Attach a 1-inch (2.5 cm) piece of cable chain to the jump ring, then wire wrap the silver charm to the end of the cable chain.

Expert Advice
Sized to Fit
The size of beads and other elements you use will affect the length of the necklace. If you need the necklace to be longer, add more beads or attach longer lengths of chain.

Chapter 6

Relics Retold

I collect old religious jewelry and relics. Small shrines and reliquaries that have been worn and touched and prayed over, rosary beads, and lockets are just a few examples of these items. I realize that some people believe religious artifacts should not be altered or changed in any manner. But my personal belief, and I am speaking only for myself, is that these beautiful objects are just…objects. If they are used in a loving manner and are worn to give a person a sense of feeling closer to someone or something they love, then this can only be a good thing.

I use portions of rosary bead chain in almost every piece I make. Mother-of-pearl rosary beads are my favorite. Over time, the beads become a murky creamy color with a texture that is not flat and smooth, but lumpy and uneven from wear. Some of my other top picks are heart-shaped connectors, lockets, and medals.

This chapter features projects made using religious artifacts as well as beads, pearls, and other jewelry elements. On one necklace, a shrine reliquary holding tiny statues makes an intriguing pendant, and a pair of earrings is made using medals and beads.

You will notice that only the shape and size of the items are called out in the Findings & Found Objects lists in this chapter. This is because the majority of the religious items are one-of-a-kind. Similar vintage and new items are easily found on the Internet and at flea markets and antique stores.

Reliquary Necklace

This necklace was constructed using pieces of a vintage French bracelet, a tintype, a dog brooch, rhinestone pieces, and a fabulous metal reliquary. Two statues rest inside the reliquary. Though the finished necklace is a bit asymmetrical, elements are repeated on both sides, helping to tie it all together.

Instructions

1. Remove the pin from the brooch using wire cutters. Smooth any rough edges with the jewelry file.

2. Cut the tintype into a 1-inch (2.5 cm) circle. Place fast-drying jewelry cement around the front edges of the tintype and adhere the rhinestone chain around the edges. Let the cement dry.

Beads
- rhinestone dangles: 3 mm (3)
- ruby gemstone beads: 5 mm (10)

Findings & Found Objects
- cable chain: 8 mm (two 2½-inch [6.4 cm] pieces; two 1-inch [2.5 cm] pieces)
- decorative pin: 25 mm
- decorative silver bracelet pieces (one 2½-inch [6.4 cm] piece; one 4½-inch [11.4 cm] piece)
- metal reliquary: 1 x 1½ inches (2.5 x 3.8 cm)
- rhinestone chain (3 inches [7.6 cm])
- rhinestone clasp: 20 x 30 mm
- rhinestone links with connectors: 12 x 20 mm (2)
- sterling silver head pins (2)
- sterling silver wire: 24-gauge
- tintype

Materials & Tools
- fast-drying jewelry cement
- jewelry file
- pliers: flat-nose, round-nose
- scissors
- wire cutters

wrap the opposite side of the ruby gemstone bead to the right side of one end of the 1-inch (2.5 cm) piece of cable chain. Wire wrap one 3 mm ruby gemstone bead on the opposite end of the chain, then wire wrap the opposite end of the ruby gemstone bead to the top right side of the clasp.

7. Repeat step 6 on the top left side of the decorative silver bracelet piece.

8. Attach one end of a rhinestone link to the top left side of the decorative pin, then connect the other side of the rhinestone link to one end of the 2½-inch (6.4 cm) piece of the decorative silver bracelet.

9. Wire wrap the top edges of the bracelet to the bottom of the rhinestone chain piece on the tintype.

10. Wire wrap one 3 mm ruby gemstone bead to the top right edge of the rhinestone chain piece on the tintype, then wire wrap the other end of the ruby gemstone bead to the end of one 2½-inch (6.4 cm) piece of cable chain. Wire wrap one 3 mm ruby gemstone bead to the opposite end of the cable chain. Wire wrap the opposite side of the ruby gemstone bead to the top left side of the clasp.

11. Repeat step 10 on the top left side of the rhinestone chain on the tintype, but this time, wire wrap the last ruby bead to the bottom left side of the clasp.

3. Wire wrap the top of the reliquary to the bottom of the decorative pin.

4. Wire wrap three rhinestone dangles and two 3 mm ruby gemstone beads to the pin as desired.

5. Attach one end of a rhinestone link to the top right side of the decorative pin, then connect the other side of the rhinestone link to one end of the 4½-inch (11.4 cm) piece of decorative silver bracelet.

6. Wire wrap one 3 mm ruby gemstone bead to the top right end of the 4½-inch (11.4 cm) piece of decorative silver bracelet, then wire

Cracker Jack & Relic Necklace

This simple necklace holds two Victorian Cracker Jack charms I bought from a very old lady at a flea market years ago. She had a binder full of charms she had saved since childhood and I spent quite a long time pouring over the pages of goodies.

Instructions

1. Wire wrap the silver reliquary pendant to the middle link on the watch fob chain. Wire wrap one mother-of-pearl bead to the right end of the watch fob chain, then make a wire-wrapped loop at the opposite end of the mother-of-pearl bead.

2. Wire wrap a 20 mm ruby gemstone bead to the wire-wrapped loop then wire wrap the opposite end of the 20 mm ruby gemstone bead to the end of the 2-inch (5.1 cm) piece of long and short cable chain.

3. Wire wrap one mother-of-pearl bead to the left end of the watch fob chain, then make a wire-wrapped loop at the opposite end of the mother-of-pearl bead.

Beads
- mother-of-pearl beads: 8 mm (2)
- ruby gemstone beads: 20 mm (1); 30 mm (1)

Findings & Found Objects
- charms (4)
- hook: 40 mm
- long and short cable chain: 12 mm (one 1½-inch [3.8 cm] piece; one 2-inch [5.1 cm] piece)
- silver reliquary pendant
- sterling silver wire: 22-gauge
- watch fob chain (8 inches [20.3 cm])

Materials & Tools
- pliers: flat-nose, round-nose
- wire cutters

4. Wire wrap the 30 mm ruby gemstone bead to the wire-wrapped loop, then wire wrap the opposite end of the 30 mm ruby gemstone bead to one end of the 1½-inch (3.8 cm) piece of long and short cable chain.

5. Wire wrap the hook to the opposite end of the 1½-inch (3.8 cm) piece of long and short cable chain.

Candy Bracelet

Each element on this bracelet is an example of my love for mixing different textures, beads, and metals. The shiny rhinestones, milky mother-of-pearl beads, and deep ruby and garnet beads combine to make a bracelet that is more like candy to the eye than rocks on a wire.

Instructions

1. Cut the tintype to fit on the back of the reliquary. Adhere the tintype to the back of the reliquary using fast-drying jewelry cement.

2. Using 24-gauge wire, wire wrap one garnet gemstone bead to the bottom right and left corners on the metal reliquary, then wire wrap the opposite end of each bead to the bottom of the rhinestone triangle pendant.

3. Using 22-gauge wire, wire wrap the mother-of-pearl oblong bead to the top of the rhinestone triangle pendant. Thread three rhinestone dangles onto the wire, then make a wire-wrapped loop at the end of the wire.

4. Using 22-gauge wire, wire wrap the crystal bead to the wire-wrapped loop, then make a wire-wrapped loop on the opposite end of the crystal bead.

5. Using 24-gauge wire, wire wrap the 12 mm ruby gemstone bead to the wire-wrapped loop, then make a wire-wrapped loop on the opposite side of the 12 mm ruby gemstone bead.

Beads
- crystal bead: 10 mm
- garnet gemstone oblong beads: 8 x 12 mm (2)
- mother-of-pearl oblong bead: 8 x 12 mm
- rhinestone bead: 15 x 20 mm
- rhinestone dangles: 3 mm (4)
- ruby gemstone beads: 3 mm (2); 12 mm (1)

Findings & Found Objects
- jump ring: 6 mm
- metal reliquary with filigree trim
- rhinestone triangle pendant
- spring ring: 16 mm
- sterling silver wire: 22-gauge, 24-gauge
- tintype

Materials & Tools
- fast-drying jewelry cement
- pliers: flat-nose, round-nose
- scissors
- wire cutters

6. Cut one 4-inch (10.2 cm) piece of 24-gauge wire and wire wrap one end of the wire to the wire-wrapped loop. In this order, thread the following onto the wire: 3 mm ruby gemstone bead, rhinestone bead, 3 mm ruby gemstone bead. Wire wrap the end of the wire to the spring ring.

7. Attach the jump ring to the back of the reliquary. Connect the spring ring to the jump ring using pliers.

Religious Connector Earrings

The exquisite details on each little element make these earrings worth talking about. When I come across small connectors, it is always a happy moment. I try to maintain a nice selection of them on hand.

Beads
- freshwater pearls: 7 mm (2)
- rhinestone dangles: 5 mm (8); 8 mm (2)
- rhinestone rondelles: 6 mm (2)
- rice pearls: 5 mm (2)

Findings & Found Objects
- cable chain: 3 mm (one ¼-inch [0.6 cm] piece; one ½-inch [1.3 cm] piece)
- head pins (2)
- silver connectors: 1-to-1 strand, 7 mm (2)
- sterling silver earring wires (2)
- sterling silver wire: 22-gauge

Materials & Tools
- pliers: flat-nose, round-nose
- wire cutters

Instructions

1. In this order, thread the following onto a head pin: freshwater pearl, rhinestone rondelle, rice pearl. Wire wrap the end of the head pin to one end of the ½-inch (1.3 cm) piece of cable chain.

2. Cut a 3-inch (7.6 cm) piece of wire. Wire wrap two 5 mm rhinestone dangles on one end, then wire wrap the other end of the wire to one end of the ¼-inch (0.6 cm) piece of cable chain.

3. Using flat-nose pliers, open the loop on one earring wire. Thread the ends of the chains onto the loop then close the loop.

4. Repeat steps 1 to 3 to make second earring.

Madonna & Child Necklace

The patina on the medal pendant gives a time-worn elegance to this necklace. The bloodstone beads give the necklace a depth of color, while the rhinestone clasp adds just a touch of sparkle.

Instructions

1. Attach the jump ring to the top of the medal. Wire wrap one bloodstone bead to the jump ring, then make a wire-wrapped loop on the other end of the bloodstone bead.

2. Wire wrap one bloodstone bead to the wire-wrapped loop, then make a wire-wrapped loop on the other end of the bloodstone bead.

3. Repeat step 2 seven times. *Note:* You now have a strand of nine wire-wrapped bloodstone beads.

4. Repeat steps 2 and 3 on left side of the medal.

5. Wire wrap one mother-of-pearl oblong bead to the wire-wrapped loop on the end of the last bloodstone bead on the right side.

Beads
- bloodstone flat oval beads: 12 mm (18)
- mother-of-pearl oblong beads: 3 x 8 mm (3)

Findings & Found Objects
- jump ring: 9 mm
- rectangular medal
- rhinestone clasp: 2-to-2 strand, 5 x 10 mm
- sterling silver wire: 24-gauge

Materials & Tools
- pliers: flat-nose, round-nose
- wire cutters

Wire wrap the opposite side of the mother-of-pearl bead to the ring on the right side of the clasp.

6. Cut one 3-inch (7.6 cm) piece of wire and wire wrap one end to the top left ring on the clasp. In this order, thread the following onto the wire: one mother-of-pearl oblong bead, the wire-wrapped loop on the end of the strand of bloodstone beads, one mother-of-pearl oblong bead. Wire wrap the end of the wire to the bottom left ring on the clasp.

Victorian Slipper Necklace

An amazing Victorian shoe cufflink is encased in the fancy reliquary pendant on this necklace. Vintage cameos and a rhinestone clasp are just the right accents.

Instructions

1. Open the reliquary. Cut a piece of velvet to fit inside; place inside the reliquary then layer the cuff link on the velvet and close the reliquary. Using a jump ring, attach a charm to the bottom edge of the reliquary.

2. Using a jump ring, attach one 2-inch (5.1 cm) piece of crystal chain to the right side of the reliquary. Using a jump ring, attach the end of the crystal chain to the top left ring of a cameo connector.

Beads
- garnet gemstone beads: 5 mm (6); 10 mm (2)

Findings & Found Objects
- cable chain: 4 mm (one 1-inch [2.5 cm] piece; two 4-inch [10.2 cm] pieces)
- cameo connectors: 2-to-2 strand, 12 mm (2)
- charms (2)
- crystal chain: various styles and sizes (four 2-inch [5.1 cm] pieces; two 4-inch [10.2 cm] pieces)
- cufflink (to fit inside reliquary)
- jump rings: 5 mm (6)
- rhinestone clasp: 2-to-2 strand, 20 mm
- round reliquary pendant with filigree edges
- sterling silver wire: 24-gauge
- velvet: 1-inch (2.5 cm) square

Materials & Tools
- pliers: flat-nose, round-nose
- scissors
- wire cutters

3. Wire wrap one 5 mm garnet gemstone bead to the top right ring of the cameo connector, then wire wrap the opposite side of the 5 mm garnet gemstone bead to the end of a 4-inch (10.2 cm) piece of crystal chain.

4. Wire wrap one 5 mm garnet gemstone bead to the end of the 4-inch (10.2 cm) piece of crystal chain. Wire wrap the opposite side of the 5 mm garnet gemstone bead to the bottom right ring on the rhinestone clasp.

5. Using a jump ring, attach one 2-inch (5.1 cm) piece of crystal chain to the top right side of the reliquary.

6. Using a jump ring, attach the end of the crystal chain to the bottom left ring of one cameo connector.

Expert Advice

Prep Work Emphasized

Before using any vintage pieces in your designs, make sure the elements can hold up to a bit of wear and tear. You may need to do some repairs to make them ready. Glue any loose stones, add new jump rings or wire-wrapped loops where needed, and work any kinks out of the chains.

7. Wire wrap one 5 mm garnet gemstone bead to the top left ring of the cameo connector, then wire wrap the opposite side of the 5 mm garnet gemstone bead to the end of a 4-inch (10.2 cm) piece of crystal chain.

8. Wire wrap one 5 mm garnet gemstone bead to the end of the 4-inch (10.2 cm) piece of crystal chain. Wire wrap the opposite side of the 5 mm garnet gemstone bead to the bottom right ring on the rhinestone clasp.

9. Repeat steps 3 to 8 to create the left side of the necklace.

10. Using a jump ring, attach one end of the 1-inch (2.5 cm) piece of cable chain to the right side of the clasp then attach a charm to the end of the cable chain.

Alternative Materials

If you have difficulty finding delicate rhinestone chains like those shown here, it is easy to make your own. Simply attach pieces of sterling silver chain to rhinestone connectors. A quick Internet search will yield rhinestone connectors in all colors, shapes, and sizes. Make sure to measure the components so your finished necklace is the desired length.

Relic & Ruby Earrings

I have included three of my favorite things on these earrings—rubies, rhinestones, and medals. Fine-gauge chain looks dainty and feminine, and enhances the delicate look.

Instructions

1. Using a jump ring, attach one medal to one end of a ½-inch (1.3 cm) piece of 4 mm cable chain.

2. Wire wrap one ruby gemstone teardrop bead to the end of a ½-inch (1.3 cm) piece of 4 mm cable chain.

3. Thread one rhinestone disco ball bead onto a head pin. Wire wrap the head pin to the end of a ½-inch (1.3 cm) piece of 2 mm cable chain.

Beads
- crystal beads: 6 mm (2)
- rhinestone disco ball beads: 6 mm (2)
- ruby gemstone teardrop beads: 12 mm (2)

Findings & Found Objects
- cable chain: 4 mm (two ½-inch [1.3 cm] pieces); 2 mm (two ½-inch [1.3 cm] pieces)
- head pins (2)
- jump rings: 5 mm (2)
- medals (2)
- sterling silver earring wires (2)
- sterling silver wire: 24-gauge

Materials & Tools
- pliers: flat-nose, round-nose
- wire cutters

4. Thread the ends of all three pieces of cable chain onto a jump ring, then attach the jump ring onto the loop on an earring wire.

5. Repeat steps 1 to 4 to make the second earring.

Bejeweled Booklet Choker

This great choker-style necklace can add a little bit of glamour to your favorite T-shirt or suit. Use any old rhinestone piece from your collection; if the piece you select does not have a center connector, you can wire wrap the pendant to the center.

Instructions

1. Using the jump ring, attach the book locket to the bottom center of the rhinestone centerpiece. Wire wrap one 6 mm garnet gemstone bead to the right side of the rhinestone centerpiece. Make a wire-wrapped loop on the opposite side of the garnet gemstone bead.

2. Wire wrap one baroque pearl to the wire-wrapped loop, then make a wire-wrapped loop on the opposite side of the baroque pearl. Wire wrap one ruby zircon gemstone bead to the wire-wrapped loop, then make a wire-wrapped loop on the opposite side of the ruby zircon bead.

3. Wire wrap one baroque pearl to the wire-wrapped loop, then make a wire-wrapped loop on the opposite side of the baroque pearl. Wire wrap one 18 mm garnet gemstone bead, then make a wire-wrapped loop on the opposite side of the garnet gemstone bead. Wire wrap one baroque pearl to the wire-wrapped loop, then make a wire-wrapped loop on the opposite side of the baroque pearl.

4. Cut one 4-inch (10.2 cm) piece of wire. Wire wrap one end of the wire to the top right loop on the clasp. In this order thread the following onto the wire: one 6 mm garnet gemstone bead, one mother-of-pearl bead, the wire-wrapped loop on the baroque pearl at the end of the chain on the right side of the necklace, one mother-of-pearl bead, one 6 mm garnet gemstone bead. Wire wrap the end of the wire to the bottom right loop on the clasp.

5. Repeat steps 2 to 4 on the left side to complete the necklace.

Beads
- baroque pearls: 12 mm (6)
- garnet gemstone beads: 6 mm (4); 12 mm (2); 18 mm (2)
- mother-of-pearl beads: 4 mm (4)
- ruby zircon gemstone beads: 12 mm (2)

Findings & Found Objects
- book locket: 20 x 25 mm
- jump ring: 7 mm
- rhinestone centerpiece (3½ inches [8.9 cm])
- rhinestone clasp
- sterling silver wire: 22-gauge

Materials & Tools
- pliers: flat-nose, round-nose
- wire cutters

This sweet little basket was in a bag of goodies sent to me from my friend in France. I love the texture of the flowers in the basket. This necklace is a great example of how to mix different sizes of chains with chunky stones.

Instructions

1. Using wire cutters, remove the pins from the back of the decorative and rhinestone pins. Smooth any rough edges with the jewelry file.

2. Cut one 5-inch (12.7 cm) piece of 22-gauge wire and make an hook closure (see Making a Hook Closure, page 23). Wire wrap the top of the pendant to the mother-of-pearl connector ring.

Beads

- garnet gemstone beads: various shapes, 15 mm (4)
- mother-of-pearl oblong bead: 6 mm x 10 mm
- mother-of-pearl round bead: 9 mm
- ruby zircon beads: 15 mm (2)

Findings & Found Objects

- crystal bead chain: 4 mm (7½ inches [19.1 cm])
- decorative pin
- jump rings: 5 mm (2)
- long and short cable chain: 8 mm (7 inches [17.8 cm])
- metal flower basket pendant
- mother-of-pearl connector ring: 18 mm
- mother-of-pearl oblong-bead rosary chain: 4 mm: (7½ inches [19.1 cm])
- rhinestone open rectangle pin: 20 mm x 25 mm
- sterling silver wire: 22-gauge, 24-gauge
- triangle connector: 2-to-1 strand

Materials & Tools

- drill bit: ½ inch (0.32 cm)
- jewelry file
- pliers: flat-nose, round-nose
- rotary drill
- wire cutters

mother-of-pearl oblong-bead rosary chain and the crystal bead chain to the bottom left side of the triangle connector.

7. Wire wrap one garnet gemstone bead to the top of the triangle connector, then make a wire-wrapped loop at the opposite side of the garnet gemstone bead.

8. In this order, wire wrap the following pieces together: garnet gemstone bead, ruby zircon bead, garnet gemstone bead, garnet gemstone bead, ruby zircon bead, mother-of-pearl oblong bead. Wire wrap the end of the mother-of-pearl oblong bead to one side of the rhinestone rectangle connector.

9. Attach the round mother-of-pearl connector to the end of the chain.

3. Drill three holes in the decorative pin as follows: one on the right, one on the left, and one in the bottom center. Each hole should be ¼ inch (0.6 cm) in from the edge.

4. Wire wrap the round mother-of-pearl bead to the bottom of the decorative pin then wire wrap the opposite end of the round mother-of-pearl bead to the bottom of the hook.

5. Wire wrap one end of the short and long cable chain to the right side of the decorative pin. Wire wrap the opposite end of the long and short cable chain to the bottom right hole of the triangle connector.

6. Wire wrap the end of the mother-of-pearl oblong-bead rosary chain and the crystal bead chain to the left side of the decorative pin. Wire wrap the opposite end of the

Alternative Materials

When I found the filigree pendant, I couldn't wait to incorporate it into a new design. Instead of searching for items that closely resemble those shown here, consider looking for unusual items that are meaningful to you. Also consider how the various elements can be attached—should the pieces be wire wrapped together, or can jump rings be used?

Amy's Advice

A Few Words of Advice

I like my workspace to inspire me, so many of my favorite elements, as well as finished pieces, are on display. It is important, however, to keep your workspace organized so the process of creating is enjoyable. These are a few favorite places to store bits and pieces:

- Cabinets with small drawers
- Cigar boxes
- Glass jars
- New plastic dividers
- Old tins
- Vintage velvet boxes

A Few of My Favorite Tips:

- When looking at jewels and gems for sale, consider the repair work required to include the pieces in your designs.

- Keep a journal handy when flea marketing and write down the price and history (if available) of each piece.

- If something looks valuable, have it appraised. You may not want to alter valuable pieces.

- Cover your workspace with parchment or paper prior to using glue or jewelry cement.

About the Author

Amy Hanna was raised in a small town in Michigan as an only child surrounded by lots of cousins and a very close-knit family. Her mother instilled in her a love of family and a fondness for objects with a storied past. Amy attended college then pursued a career as a flight attendant, which fulfilled her desire to travel and explore. After living in various places across the country, Amy relocated to Southern California with her husband, Todd. Her most cherished accomplishment is being a mother to her son, Bailey, and twin daughters, Isabella and Sophia. Amy has appeared on television craft shows and is highly sought-after as a teacher at industry shows. Her work has been featured in a variety of magazines and can be found in private collections around the globe. To see more of Amy's work, visit www.amyhanna.etsy.com and amyhanna.typepad.com.

Acknowledgments

I would first like to thank my three beautiful children—Bailey, Isabella, and Sophia, for telling their friends that their mommy is an artist. Nothing matters more to me than the three of you believing in me. Bailey, thank you for encouraging me through this whole process and always loving me, even when I was a stressed-out maniac. Bella and Sophia, I cannot wait to see what amazing artists you will turn out to be.

I would like to thank my husband, Todd, who works endless hours but always has time to drill a hole for me with his oh-so-steady hands. Your love and support through every bit of life makes me a better person.

To my sweet parents, who I am so very blessed to have. Thank you for loving the kids so much and giving so unselfishly of yourselves. You have been my extra hands through this time. Thank you, Mom, for always letting me know that anything is possible. One of the main reasons I wanted to write this book was to encourage people the same way you have always encouraged me.

To my granny, who taught me the art of creating and to take pride in my creations. I will always remember the love in her eyes when she gave someone a gift she had made by hand.

To my aunts, for always teaching me to see the beauty in things, even those things that are not considered beautiful.

Thank you to Wanda for investing so much time in me, to Polly for antiquing with me until we wanted to drop from exhaustion and for all of our deep talks, and to Judy for loving me so sweetly.

Thank you to Bonnie for always making such beautiful things, to Shirley for your kindness and generosity, to Billie for always giving me something out of love, and to Betsy, who will get up at the crack of dawn and rent a moving van to go to a flea market with me.

To Lisa, thank you for all of our inspiring talks and for sharing creative dreams.

To Pam, I will be forever in your debt because you taught me to value creativity. Thank you for not quitting and for not letting me fire you. You have truly been a blessing to me. You are one of the most creative people I know and I feel blessed to call you a friend. Your loyalty is so appreciated. I love you and look forward to our next adventure.

To Denise, thank you for not letting me pass up this opportunity and for all the years of love. To my dear friend Carole, you are an incredible artist and I thank you for lovingly taking me under your wings.

Melanie, Charmane, Diane, and Julie, thank you for long talks and for always cheering me on. I love you girls. Thanks for wearing my jewels so well, and for all of the good times. Most of all, thanks for reminding me to praise God in all things.

Liz, thank you for all of your hard work. You have been an incredible friend. I am so excited that we get to experience this together. I love seeing you shine.

Thank you Tamara for all of the early morning search-and-rescue missions, years of creating, and friendship. To Denise, for encouraging me to do this book and for lending Margaret to me.

Vicki, thanks for always encouraging me. I miss you. Thanks to Corey, Coco, and Freddie for sharing all of your wonderful treasures.

To my editor, Rebecca, thank you for your patience with me. Your mellow disposition was my cup of soothing tea. I thank you and Eileen for believing in me and giving me this opportunity. I appreciate all of your hard work and wish you many blessings.

Index